MW00592406

Sometimes it Takes Three Hearts

By

Vin LoPresti

and

Chad Boily

BRIARWOOD PUBLICATIONS, INCORPORATED

First Published 1999
Briarwood Publications & Sassy Cat Books, Inc.
150 West College Street
Rocky Mount, Virginia 24151

Vin LoPresti & Chad Boily

Sometimes it Takes Three Hearts
ISBN: 1-892614-18-9

Manufactured in the United States of America.

Printed by Briarwood Publications, Inc.

Acknowledgements

The authors wish to express their deep appreciation to the following individuals:

- The immediate and extended families of Robert Ouellette and Lorraine (LaPlante) Ouellette for their willingness to share their recollections, their encouragement, and most of all, for their love.

- Special thanks to Jim Ouellette for computer support, to Ann (Ouellette) LoPresti for her great patience and to Louise (Ouellette) Boily for her unwavering courage.

- The physicians, nurses, pharmacists and staff of Children's Hospital, Boston, Maine Medical Center, Portland and Central Maine Medical Center, Lewiston, for their skill and compassion.

- Special thanks to Doctors Perry, Smoot, Del Nido, McFaul and Hourihan.

- The family of heart-transplant-recipient Owen Stacy, one of Chad's inspirations and a dear friend, who regrettably passed away during the fall of 1998.

Introduction

Hyper-Extended Family & the Power of Positive Energy

"The power of prayer," "the power of positive thinking," "good energy," "God's grace": For centuries, we have postulated the existence of an ethereal potency that despite its many names, has never been well-understood in scientific terms.

On the surface, this is a book about one child's struggle to live, about the triumphs of medical science in sustaining a young life teetering at the edge of extinction. But at a deeper level, it also chronicles the action of that ephemeral force, arising in this instance from the collective thought forms of literally thousands of people who have known or known of Chad Boily at some moment in their lives. In a real sense, this collection of minds—and hearts—constitutes Chad's hyper-extended family, and in that sense, this is a book about genuine "family values."

I first became acquainted with the nucleus of Chad's sizable biological family during the summer of 1984. I was deeply in love with Chad's aunt, my future wife, Ann, and the urgency of my affection compelled me to detour to the French-Canadian Mecca of Lewiston, Maine on my return trip to Boston from a solo hiking tour of Acadia National Park.

I spotted Chad kneeling in the sand at the edge of a lake, tightly clutching a hefty bullfrog, his attention focused on a sunfish swimming near shore.

Ann explained: "There aren't many bass left in the lake, but Chad's always looking for them."

When he stood to greet the visitor, I was presented with a small, frail-looking, frog-infatuated four-year-old with a grayish skin tone and a huge surgical scar down the center of his chest.

Almost immediately, I became aware of a presence much larger and healthier than Chad's physical being. It began with a genuinely cheerful smile and bursts of laughter that seemed to bubble-up from somewhere much deeper than the core of his diminutive body. And like the catchiest of sing-along tunes, every joyful sound and expression spread rapidly to those frequently around him—his mom and sister, his grandparents, "Memé" and "Pepé," his great-grandfather, his six aunts and uncles, and his grandmother's numerous siblings, their children and grandchildren. How one small child with a defective heart could simultaneously shift the mood of so many distinct individuals of different generations was a phenomenon that I would only come to fully appreciate years later.

Within a few hours at his grandparents' small, rustic lakeside camp, I had become one of the captivated. From that first proudly displayed frog to his first request to "pull my finger, Vinny," I realized that the fragility of Chad's biological life was somehow compensated for by a psychological energy that sustained his moment-to-moment existence. My natural inclination to feel sorry for him evaporated in the sunshine of the love radiating from the Ouellette and LaPlante families. I felt myself drawn into that group energy, an ongoing celebration of life, and soon, my own inadequately expressed love for Chad became part of the powerful synergy that constantly illuminated his spirit.

Back home in Boston the following day, I recall several phone conversations with close friends, during which I couldn't help but relate the story of the four-year-old I had just met. It was remarkable how quickly my friends responded with a deep concern for someone who was essentially a stranger to them. Whether it was my enthusiasm or simply their own empathy for a young child burdened with disabilities that no young child should have to bear, they were instantly recruited into Chad's army of well-wishers. I had unwittingly established my own sub-branch of the extended network that in one way or another prayed for Chad. Twelve years later, one of those friends would express the phenomenon to me in this fashion: "I wouldn't even know him if I saw him on the street . . . can't tell you what color his hair is or if he's black, white or yellow; but I've been sending him good energy since the first day you told me about him."

To appreciate the extent of this network, Chad's hyper-extended family, consider that Chad's biological family comprises several hundred individuals originating in the twin mill-cities of Lewiston and Auburn, Maine, but subsequently dispersed throughout New England, the United States and beyond. Imagine that something akin to the response I observed among my own friends was also transpiring among the friends and acquaintances of each of those individuals. Add the many people whom Chad encountered during his several extended hospitalizations, and the results, in terms of sheer numbers, are staggering. As expressed by Chad's sister, Amy: "There seemed to be so many people who knew what was going on. We've had people whom we've met once or twice in passing and said, 'Hi, how are you,' send cards, and we don't even remember their names."

It is a fundamental premise of this book that Chad's life was and is a miracle, or if you prefer, a series of minor miracles. Without the enormous spiritual energy that sustained him and his immediate family through crisis after crisis, without the saving grace that manifested itself in a diversity of individuals—medical and non-medical alike—Chad might never have lived long enough to feel a normal heart pumping smoothly behind his breastbone. At every turn of his difficult life, we see the hand of God intervening, often in incomprehensible ways, but always, ultimately, in Chad's behalf. This then is a story of abiding love, tough enough to endure more than a decade of battles, potent enough to compensate in spirit what was lacking in flesh.

CHAPTER ONE:
Donor

"*D*onor," I shouted, flailing my arms as I *spazzed* around the second floor of my house. Inside my chest, I felt the alien *gwoosh, gwoosh, gwoosh* of my Fontan heart, a patched-together pump that had been keeping me alive since I was nine. It was a heart whose beat my mom swore she could hear from two feet away in a quiet room.

Puzzled expressions on their faces, a group of visiting friends split my bedroom. They were stranged-out by my antics; worried that I might be going *postal.*

I understood why they thought I had finally flipped-out. For as much as they cared, there was really no way they could understand my craze. Every time I repeated that fateful word, "donor," I got a roller-coaster rush.

I had just ended the most important phone call of my life, a short conversation with one of my two new cardiologists at Boston's Children's Hospital, the awesome Doctor Stan Perry. At first, I thought it was just another check-up call, another of the many times during my three-month wait that Children's would phone to see how I was doing.

No one ever needed to tell Doc Perry to "chill." He was a cool dude, very together. "Hi Chad, how are you feeling?" he asked.

"Not too bad, Doc Perry," I said.

"Do you have a cold or any other type of infection?"

I began to wonder. Usually, he asked about my blood oxygen or my energy level. Why, suddenly, was the question about infections?

"No, I don't, doc. I'm cool with colds."

"Well, in that case, is your mother there?" he asked.

"No, she's out tonight," I said.

It had been three months since my mom, Louise, had allowed herself a night out with her fiancé. Brian had been asked to host a Blue Cross/Blue Shield Christmas party, and he was the major after-dinner speaker. Pagers in hand, Brian and Mom reluctantly left me home, the first evening since mid-August that one or both of them had not been there with me. They trusted my friends to keep me company without letting me burn myself out. And there wasn't a heck of a lot of energy standing between me and overdone toast. It was only three days since my last hospital stay, and the discharge order said it all: "Very little ambulation."

"I know where my parents can be reached, Doc Perry," I said. "You want me to call them?"

"Yes, I think you'd better have them call my beeper number, Chad," he said. "We have a possible donor."

What a rush; the words *reverbed* through my brain like a butt-kicking guitar solo through digital delay.

I knew I had to keep it together, but the moment I hung up the phone, I began bawling tears of joy. A new life was now closer than it had ever been. I wanted to tell everybody around me, but between the adrenaline high and my bogus energy, I was completely blown-away. My mouth and throat felt like cat furballs. I bounced around the house repeating that one awesome word: "Donor."

Two of my friends threw-out their hands for support and led me back to my bedroom. Gently, they lowered me onto my bed. "You gotta chill, Chad," my friend Kim said. "Remember . . . very little ambulation."

"Ambulation . . . ambulation," my friend Max repeated. I could tell he thought it was a cool word.

"As in movement, dork," my friend Colin said.

"I know, I know," Max said to Colin. He shook his head.

"Dude, you look like you swallowed your harp," Max said to me. "How 'bout hummin' a few riffs."

I usually caught-a-chuckle from Max's one-liners, but at that moment, my brain was buzzing with only one thought. "I need to call my mom," I said.

My friend Steve handed me the phone. I could barely concentrate on dialing the number.

"Chad, what's wrong?" my mother asked, when she heard my crazed breathing. The woman who called her to the phone had already told her that it was an emergency, and naturally, Mom thought my heart was failing again. She figured I was headed for another hospital stay right after the last one.

"Oh my God, what's wrong?" Mom repeated. "Your breathing sounds terrible."

"Mom, please come home now," I mumbled.

Whatever I said next was obviously a babble; an L-twelver.

"I can't understand what you're saying, honey; you've got to calm down," my mother said.

Mom remembers hearing me draw a long deep breath before I shouted: "Mom . . . we've got a donor."

She began to cry. "I'm on my way . . . on my way, Chad. We'll be right there."

My mother later told me that my words sent a chill from her toes to the tip of her hair. In her rush to tell Brian, she also made a spectacle of herself. Waving her hands, she ran back into the banquet room, calling out: "We have a donor."

Most of the guests were clueless about the strange hysterical woman. So Brian jumped in, apologized for having to split early and asked a friend to explain Mom's behavior to the guests. Grasping her hand, Brian led her to their car. I have no doubt that if it had been dinner at the White House, their reaction would have been exactly the same.

I turned down the *Gorilla Biscuits* CD and tried to chill. Then it hit me: I needed to call my Uncle Bob. A major dude in my life, Doc Bob never let me down. He left his house right away—to keep me company and keep an eye on my failing heart.

"This is awesome, dude," I heard Max say. "But you need to chill until your unk gets here. We're gonna split so you can cop some rack-time." He motioned to the others.

"Yeah, Chad," Kim said. "Major chill."

I didn't want them to leave, but I knew they were right.

"Cool," I said. "Catch you later."

As I struggled to get my brain in gear, I knew I had to spread the word to my family. It was the natural thing to do. They had seen me through so much, and I had to share this with them now. I phoned my Uncle David, one of my mom's two youngest brothers, with whom my sister and I had grown up. Between David and Bob's wife, my Aunt Claire, I knew they would broadcast the news.

While I waited for Uncle Bob to arrive, I shuffled around the second floor, desperately trying to concentrate on packing my list of stuff for a hospital stay. *Over two hours and a hundred miles to Boston,* I kept thinking. Boston—where my new heart was hopefully still beating strongly and steadily.

Every activity, every thought became a battle. I was trying to run, but I couldn't muster the energy. *Weesh as usual,* I thought. I felt like I couldn't breathe, yet I was hyperventilating from the adrenaline. A donor had been found, but that meant someone had died—maybe someone young like me.

The doorbell rang. W*hat now*? It seemed too soon for Uncle Bob's arrival. But I'd completely lost track of time.

I hobbled down the smooth, blond-oak staircase and cracked open the front door. Colin, Max, Kim, and Steve were smiling, but I could tell they were still flipped-out.

With all the love showered on me by my family, I had still always been a *zeke*. Until I'd met these guys, I'd never had any really close friends. And suddenly, it dawned on me that so many things were changing at once. I realized that I had already received many of the blessings of a new life, and tonight was hopefully going to be the final gift of God's grace that would finish the picture. I prayed I would know how to deal with it all—to hang tough.

"Dude," Colin said. "We couldn't just leave you solo at a time like this. We felt like we were copping-out on you."

"We promise we'll stay out of the way . . . make like invisible dudes," Max added. "But we have to be here with you . . . to bring you a glass of water . . . spin some tunes, or . . . do anything you need help with."

I hugged them all. Feeling like you were loved was never played-out.

Uncle Bob arrived a few minutes later, and he examined me before helping me climb the stairs and allowing me to finish packing. My mind was easily distracted, jumping from the good-natured conversation floating up from the living room, to the background noise of the TV in the kitchen, to the new *Queers* CD Max had spun in my player. The *Queers* were epic.

But there was only one sound I really wanted to hear— the crunch of tires rolling over the loose ice in our driveway.

Finally, I heard that awesome sound.

"Chad, they're here," Bob shouted from the base of the stairs.

After hugs all around, reality zonked us. It was seven-thirty, and Doc Perry had told my mother to zone-in on ten p.m. as our arrival time. After years of driving to and from Boston, we had learned that we could usually depend on the worst traffic in God's universe. "City of gridlock, bottleneck of America," one of my uncles always said. The possibility that I might be late for my new heart suddenly rattled all our brains. We hustled into Brian's black and gold Grand Cherokee.

Clicking on his emergency flashers, Brian gunned the Jeep onto the Maine Turnpike. Safely on the highway, he picked up the cell phone and dialed the state police. For one of the few times I remember, there was almost panic in his voice as he explained the situation.

"How you doin' back there, boss?" he asked me, after clicking off the cell phone.

"I'm cool, boss," I said.

"What did they say?" Mom asked nervously.

"That they couldn't sanction speeding, but they understood our situation," Brian said. "I think they're telling us to use our own best judgment."

I felt a surge of acceleration and watched as the speedometer needle climbed toward eighty. *We're gonna make it*, I told myself.

As we sped down the turnpike, I couldn't help zoning-out about the past four months. I had lived a Jello-brain life. Unable to attend school, I'd been forced to drop three classes to focus my limited energy on the three required ones I'd need to graduate on time. I really enjoyed those three lost classes, but fulfilling requirements for graduation and getting into college had to be my priority. After many years of a spotty relationship with school, I had finally reached a point where learning new stuff was awesome—at a time when my heart had become too *weesh* to allow me to attend.

The arrival of my home tutor had become the high point of each endless day alone. Some nights, my friends would come by to pick-up my spirits. But every morning, I faced another long day of exhausted boredom; another day of struggling to get out of bed; of fighting for every breath.

The fact that I was hardly sleeping didn't help. I'd found out what many congestive heart failure patients already knew. A hard-core itching sensation zonked me every night, making a good night's sleep almost impossible. It felt like fleas were burrowing into every inch of my skin.

Yet, as bogus as those days were, the alternative was major bunk. The Special Care Unit of Maine Medical Center had some awesome docs and nurses, but during those months on the transplant list, I had spent far too many days in a hospital bed. We called each of those hospital visits a "recharge." It was my mom's way of being hopeful, of expressing the chance that some magic spell could be cast over my failing heart to jump-start its ability to move blood around my body.

Only later would I realize that those hospital stints on intravenous drugs were just a rest period. The drugs acted on my blood vessels to take the strain off my failing heart muscle, giving it a temporary boost so my blood oxygen level could climb a few percent. But the moment I left the hospital, I was immediately in danger of falling back in.

The stench of sewage stabbed at my nostrils and zonked me back to the present. There was no mistaking the paper-mill waste of Westbrook, and to our left, just beyond, glared the intense lights of Maine Mall with its acres of car dealerships. We had reached Portland, Maine's largest city. We were halfway from home to the New Hampshire border.

Come on, Brian, crank this baby, I thought.

I shifted my mind away from thoughts of the recent past by zoning-in on my mantra. I recited it to myself every day, used it to pump myself up: "I'm going to have better days, days when I'll be able to do things again, maybe even things I've never done before," I whispered.

And as we sped past the twin glass towers of the South Portland Sheraton Tara, I added an extra reassurance: "So many people are praying for me; God loves me and is keeping me alive for a reason."

One way or another, it looked like the revolving door sweeping me in and out of the Maine Medical Center Special Care Unit might be about to stop spinning. The worst part about that situation had been the catch-22 of transplant listing. For being in the hospital—under treatment for a life-threatening condition—made me a higher priority as a transplant recipient. The moment I returned home, my position on that hazy "list" automatically slid a few places. And nobody could tell us how many.

It was a major horror-show. And the worst part was what it did to my mom. One night, I had found her crying alone in the kitchen as she cleaned up after dinner. Seeing her in tears was no surprise; after sixteen years of struggling to do everything in her power to keep me alive, a good cry helped her blow-off some of the stress. But this particular night felt different.

"Mom, what's wrong?" I asked.

"I just heard about a car accident on the turnpike, Chad," she sobbed. "A seventeen-year-old girl was killed. And I felt terrible for her and her family. But then . . . I wondered whether she could be the source of a heart for you. I looked in the mirror and felt so guilty, I wanted to smack myself."

"It's okay, Mom," I said, hugging her. I couldn't stand

to see her suffer like that.

Brian's voice snapped me out of my daydream. He was talking into the car phone again. When I looked up, we were crossing the bridge from Maine into New Hampshire. The dashboard clock told me it was almost a quarter to nine. If everything went well, we had a good chance of making Boston by ten.

"They said just about the same thing as the Maine State police," Brian said to my mother. "I'm just going to keep cruising until we hit Mass."

"How do you feel, Chad?" Mom asked.

I smiled. "Like I want to get there right now, Mom."

Usually the fifteen miles of Route 95 along the short New Hampshire seacoast seemed to go by in no time at all. But tonight, the same distance felt endless. Portsmouth, Rye, Hampton and Seabrook, and finally, we crossed into Massachusetts.

Brian dialed the car phone for the third time. This time, the conversation sounded different.

"Almost back to Ninety-five?" Brian said. I could tell he was really bent out of shape.

He covered the phone's mouthpiece, glanced over at my mother and shook his head. "They said there's a fire on Route One . . . we'll never get through."

"This is unbelievable," Mom said, her fingers tearing at the handhold above her door. "What are we going to do?"

My stomach felt like the snake scene from *Raiders of the Lost Ark*. Route One was the most direct way to get from Interstate 95 into Boston. An old two-lane, traffic-snarled road lined with mini-malls and restaurants, it was the only way we were sure of, the one we'd traveled enough times to make it automatic. And anyone who knows Boston also knows that finding a new route on the spur of the moment is like boogying through a minefield without a map.

I could tell what was going through my mother's mind, because the same thought also zipped through my own. *Oh God*, we were thinking, *after all this, could it be that I was going to miss my chance at a new life because of a stupid Boston traffic jam?*

Brian quickly made the only cool decision. He asked the police to phone for an ambulance to meet us near the Interstate 95/Route 1 interchange.

A half-mile later, our speed dropped to thirty, then to twenty. Suddenly, we were crawling along at just a few miles per hour, approaching the back end of what must have been a ten-mile backup.

"Over there," my mother said, pointing to the right.

We spotted the flashing lights on an exit ramp. Brian weaved over to the right lane and squeezed his way off the exit.

Within minutes, Mom and I were in the ambulance. The ambulance driver was awesome: Siren blaring, he rock-and-rolled his way through the traffic jam.

I lifted my head to look out the rear window. Brian was on our tail like a NASCAR driver drafting; it was like his front bumper was magnetized to the ambulance's rear.

"Don't worry, Chad, we're going to make it," Mom said. I smiled. I didn't believe that God was going to let me down at the last minute.

My thoughts shifted to the awesome medical team waiting for me at Children's. Compared to the chilled-out Doctor Perry, my other cardiologist, Doctor Leslie Smoot was an intense woman with short salt-and-pepper hair, who had done her best to form a bond with me from the first time we had met back in August. "That's a heck of a platinum," she had said when she first saw my bleach-blond punk cut, but the way she zinged me about it always made me feel like it was cool with her.

"Tell you what I'm gonna do, Chad," she had said on my last visit to Children's. "When you get a heart, I promise to color my hair the shade of your choice."

For some reason, it was Doctor Smoot's vow that was on my mind as the ambulance skirted the front wave of the traffic jam and sped toward the Tobin Bridge and Boston just beyond. It was the message behind her promise that made it so important to me. She was telling me that my hair color wasn't important. What mattered to her was a healthy heart beating inside my body. I wondered if she'd keep her promise, but even if she didn't, she had already shown me what I needed to know—that she wasn't about to judge me because of the way I looked. It made me think about what awesome people my friends were, and how much crap they took from some adults because of their clothes or the color of their hair.

"We're almost there, Chad; we're going to make it, honey," my mother said, squeezing my *weesh* left hand. "Are you okay?"

"I'm psyched, Mom," I said, feeling another rush of adrenaline. She had caught me thinking about my surgeon. It was mind-boggling how anyone could take on that kind of responsibility—to stand in the doorway between life and death. I respected him for his courage.

The ambulance scooted through the light traffic on the local streets. As we pulled up to the hospital, I saw Brian's Jeep turn the corner toward the parking lot across Brookline Avenue. He was still with us.

In no time at all, I was in my room in the Cardiac Intensive Care Unit. It was a small space with glass walls and no privacy. As nurses hustled around me preparing and inserting IVs, Doctor Perry gave me the bad news. There was a delay harvesting the donor's heart, because all the other organs were also usable for transplantation, and the heart had to be left in place to circulate blood through them. My new heart would be the last organ harvested.

Since no one knew exactly when the heart would arrive, the docs had to prepare my body to receive it at any time. That meant I had to take the first dose of what I already knew would probably be a lifetime dance with Cyclosporine, the anti-rejection drug that had made organ transplantation much more possible.

That first dose of Cyclosporine made me feel like waves of hot oil were being flushed through my body. Since I was still riding my last adrenaline high and was wide-awake, I found it impossible to relax.

My own heart sounded sicker with each *gwooshy* beat, and for an instant, I flashed on the possibility that it could give-out at any second. But Mom's gentle fingers stroking my forehead and Brian's strong grip on my shoulder pulled me through.

Doc Perry took one look at me and prescribed some Valium. By the time they repeated the surgical prep at two a.m., I was mega-relaxed, almost Jello. But I was still awake enough to talk with my nurses on the trip to the operating room.

The O.R. was jumping when we arrived, and only the clock on the wall reminded us that it was actually the middle of the night.

As they lifted my body onto the operating table, I looked up into the soft hazel eyes of one of my nurses. I began to cry—for I was minutes from becoming a new person. She returned the glance, and our eyes stayed locked for what must have been almost a minute.

"Are you scared, Chad?" she asked.

I shook my head. "No, not at all. I'm happy."

The next thing I knew, I was asleep, and I remember only one dream image from that long night in the O.R. I was a little boy again, kneeling in the sand at the edge of Allen Pond, holding a frog with my two little hands. And behind me, I heard the familiar voice of my grandmother. "How are you feeling today, Chad?" she was asking.

"I feel fine, Memé, I feel fine," I answered.

CHAPTER TWO: A Whole Soul With Half a Heart

I was twenty-three years old and in perfect health, and the only unusual feature of the pregnancy was its stillness. Unlike his sister, Amy, Chad was deathly quiet in the womb. But as I'd learned from my own mother, I tried to be positive about it. Perhaps my baby was secure and happy inside me.

I later came to realize that Chad's pre-natal silence was an omen of muscular disabilities that I couldn't even imagine at the time. Beginning with his heart muscle and ending with the smallest muscle in his body, Chad was already showing us the lack of energy that would become a signature of his childhood.

During Chad's first week home, I believed I had been blessed with a normal, healthy child. After a glitch-free vaginal birth, the obstetrician gave Chad a good Apgar score, and we were discharged from the hospital in less than three days. The only hint of a problem was the continuation of the inactivity that Chad had shown in the womb. His main activity during that first week of life was sleeping.

"There's no reason for concern; babies do that," Chad's pediatrician said when I phoned about my anxieties.

Questioning authority figures was not something that came easily. I was a housewife and mother, with a twelfth-grade education, who sewed and baked to earn extra money.

It never dawned on me that the pediatrician might be overlooking something.

The pattern continued during Chad's second week home, and my mother urged me to keep bugging the doctor. But I didn't want to be a nuisance, and I suppose I was avoiding the gut feeling that something really *was* wrong. It was mid-May and spring was showing her face in central Maine, the warm rays finally chasing the last of winter's chill from the soil. The tulips were blooming and the maple buds were bursting into tufts of emerald. I had a new son and there was every reason to be grateful for life. Why would I want to spoil it with thoughts of illness?

My illusions began to crumble. One afternoon, I sat by his crib and watched him closely for what must have been twenty minutes. His little chest heaved continually—without so much as a split second's rest. I couldn't imagine how he could keep it up without his muscles cramping. My son was struggling just to breathe, I realized.

I felt overwhelmed with fear. I phoned my mother and asked her to come over. Thankfully, she lived only two short blocks away and appeared at my door within minutes.

"Mom, he seems to be breathing so fast," I said. "I can't remember if Amy breathed like that or not."

"My gosh, Louise, I don't think I ever saw a baby breathe like that," my mom said. "You've got to bring him to the doctor's."

My mother had raised seven children, and her opinion carried a lot of weight. I phoned the pediatrician's office and tried to explain what we were observing.

"Perhaps it just seems like your baby's breathing rapidly," the nurse said. "Newborns do . . . naturally . . . have a higher respiratory rate."

Foolishly, I accepted her explanation. After all, she was a nurse; she had studied many years for her impressive knowledge. Me, I was just a blue-collar nobody; a paranoid parent. I hung up the phone. Still skeptical, my mother threw me a look of disbelief before leaving. I could tell that she thought me foolish.

Fortunately, my friend Cathy—a registered nurse—paid us a visit just a few days later. As we sipped tea at the kitchen table, I noticed that Cathy's attention seemed focused on Chad as he napped in his crib.

Suddenly, Cathy rose from her chair and inched closer to him. Resting her hand lightly on his chest, she leaned over and positioned her ear close to his tiny face.

"Louise, call the doctor and tell them you have a friend who's a nurse and who also thinks his breathing is labored. *Insist* that they examine Chad." Cathy's tone sent a shiver down my back, a twinge of terror that rattled in my voice as I demanded a doctor's appointment.

The next morning, I sat alone in the pediatrician's waiting room. Every so often, I glanced around at the other mothers, occupying my mind by trying to guess the ages of their babies. But each time I glanced toward the reception desk, I noticed the nurse's eyes riveted on Chad resting in my arms.

After a few minutes, she came over to me. "Why don't you bring Chad into the examining room now, Mrs. Boily," she said.

I pointed around the room. "But all these people are ahead of me."

"I know. But I think the doctor needs to see Chad right away," she said. "I don't like the way his skin looks."

I suppose I had noticed that Chad's cheeks weren't really rosy. But seeing him each day, I couldn't be sure, and I thought I remembered that Amy's color had also changed over the first month of her life.

The doctor didn't try to hide his concern as he examined

Chad. "He has to have an X-ray," the pediatrician said.

The nurse immediately phoned Lewiston's Central Maine Medical Center and handed me a stack of forms to bring to the Radiology Unit.

C.M.M.C. was far from the prettiest place in Lewiston. It was located downtown, in the most congested part of the city; near the old mills where my mom had stitched leather purses to help my father support their seven children when his three jobs just weren't enough. The buildings were dirty brown, the parking impossible. As I circled the block looking for a space, my mind got locked into a repeating cycle of thoughts: *Why did I come alone? Something is very strange here. Two weeks ago, the hospital sent me home believing I had a healthy baby. Why did I come alone? Oh God, please help me; I'm so scared.*

In the Radiology waiting room, I found a phone and dialed the number of a friend's house, trying to reach my husband who was supposedly there building a garage. But there was no answer. Frantically, I tried several other friends, but no one seemed to know where Amos was. I wasn't surprised. A pattern of non-communication had crept into our marriage over those years, and my husband was often hard to find. I later learned that he was playing Frisbee on the Maine seacoast at Old Orchard Beach.

Alone and scared, I began to cry as much for my own situation as for my baby's. I longed for a tender arm around my shoulders. I craved the family support that throughout my life had been there for me at times like these; an encouraging love and determination that had gotten us through so many crises.

Out of nowhere, a woman I didn't recognize sat beside me and offered me a tissue. "Aren't you Lorraine Ouellette's oldest daughter?" she said.

"Yes, I'm Louise," I nodded. "How do you know

Mom?" I figured it was either from church or from my mother's many musical activities within the community.

"I'm a friend of your Aunt Simone's," she said. "You look like you need a strong shoulder. Would you like me to find her for you? I know she's in the hospital visiting a mutual friend."

"Oh . . . yes . . . please," I said.

At that awful moment, God blessed me with the company of my mom's youngest sister, one of the most upbeat members of my large family. It was a small miracle that I have never stopped being thankful for.

Simone arrived just as three male physicians converged on me, and she literally held me up as we listened to their unbelievable message.

"We've just ordered an ambulance to take you to Portland," the oldest-looking of the physicians said. I knew that he meant Maine Medical Center, the largest and best-equipped hospital in the state.

In spite of the late-June humidity, my mouth suddenly felt like this was the driest, coldest mid-winter day. My lips and tongue were so parched that I could barely speak. "I don't understand . . . why can't you treat him here?" I rasped.

One of the younger cardiologists answered. He was a man who had obviously never developed a skill for sanding the sharp edges off horrendous news. "I don't think you appreciate how terribly ill your baby is, Mrs. Boily," he said. "The x-ray of Chad's heart indicates that we're not equipped to treat such a serious condition here."

That ambulance ride would turn out to be the first in an endless line of visits to M.M.C.'s Pediatric Cardiology Unit, and it was one of the longest hours of my life. Without Aunt Simone by my side, I doubt I would have held together. With every mile came another rush of guilt that it was my failure to act promptly—to insist that the pediatrician see

Chad—which had caused a more minor problem to mushroom into what was now something major.

Simone clung to my arm while the M. M. C. cardiologists gave us their diagnosis. Chad was suffering from congestive heart failure. Fluids were accumulating in his organs, especially in his enlarged liver.

My own heart felt like the molten solder my husband used to seal the joints in boilers. It was only Aunt Simone's bear hug that prevented my body from collapsing to the floor.

Simone left to take care of her own children, when my husband arrived a few minutes later. The moment Amos opened his mouth, I heard the disbelief in his voice. And as he sometimes did, Amos felt he had to find somebody to blame. Shaking his head, he insisted that this had to be a mistake. Why would C.M.M.C. have discharged mother and child two days after birth if anything had been wrong with Chad?

We were taken to the office of Doctor Richard McFaul. A pleasant man of average height with thinning brown hair and glasses, Doctor McFaul tried to explain what the medical team had discovered so far. "We've admitted Chad to the hospital," he said. "His heart is very enlarged, as is his liver, and the blood vessels in his lungs are abnormally swollen. His heart is failing to circulate enough blood . . . failing to get enough oxygen to his other organs. In other words, he's in congestive heart failure. We've put him on Lanoxin, a drug that will help his heart muscle pump blood more efficiently."

"Oh merciful God, this is unbelievable," I muttered, feeling inadequate to follow Doctor McFaul's explanation. But my baby was obviously very sick, and I was determined to understand as much as I could. That day began my long-term education in cardiology.

"You gotta be kiddin' me. That's an old peoples'

disease, isn't it? He's just a baby, for Chrissake," Amos said to the doctor.

"I'm truly sorry, Mister Boily. Congestive heart failure can occur in anyone whose heart is failing to circulate enough blood," Doctor McFaul explained. "To add to our problems, Chad is in danger of suffering irreversible lung damage. We've scheduled a cardiac catheterization for tomorrow morning. It's possible we may need to send him to Boston for surgery."

I could tell that my husband was on the verge of tears. "Oh Jesus, not my son," he said, reaching for the cigarettes in his pocket. He bolted for the door of Chad's room.

Excusing myself, I charged after him, catching up in the sunny lobby outside the Special Care Unit.

"Where do you think you're going?" I asked.

"I need a cigarette," Amos said.

"First, I can't reach you because you're fooling around with your friends when you're supposed to be working. Now, you're running out on me when I need your support the most."

"Give me a break, Louise. I'm tired of gettin' ragged-on for hangin' out with my friends."

"To hell with your friends," I said, pointing back toward Chad's room. "That's your son in there."

"Yeah . . . my son with an old man's heart. Thanks a lot, God."

"Don't you dare second-guess God. There's always a reason for what he gives us," I said.

"Yeah, He's kickin' my butt again. When you said you'd marry me, I asked Him for a son. This is what I get."

"He's a baby with a sick heart, and he's gonna need all the love we can give him."

"Just let me have a smoke, okay?" Amos said. He pushed through a set of glass doors and lit a cigarette.

I couldn't really blame my husband for his reaction.

The shock of discovering that his supposedly healthy new son was actually mortally ill was unlike anything he had ever coped with. He needed to vent his desperation as anger, while I just wanted to hide in a dark room and bawl my eyes out.

But I calmed myself down, and for Chad's sake, returned to Doctor McFaul's office to ask whatever questions I could think of. If our family squabble had affected him, the doctor never let me know it. I immediately developed a great respect for him.

"Doctor, if his heart's so big, why can't it do the job?" I began.

"Several reasons," Doctor McFaul said. "We believe that the left side of Chad's heart . . . normally the stronger pump, is underdeveloped and weak. We also think there might be a canal . . . a hole . . . between the left and right sides. The cardiac catheterization will give us a more complete picture."

"Doctor," I said, feeling the tears flooding my eyes. "Is my baby going to die?"

Doctor McFaul held up his hand. "There's no need to entertain those thoughts," he said. "He's very sick, but right now, he's stable . . . and we've treated children with these defects before."

"How could this happen?" I asked.

"Sometimes, one or more organs fail to develop their complete structure during pregnancy," Doctor McFaul said. "Often, it occurs simply as an accident, a developmental anomaly."

Ten years later, the family would contain a physician, a pharmacist and a biologist to fall back on for explanations, but in June of 1980, we were on our own, trying to translate the meaning of a foreign language, with minds shocked by the completely unexpected. The following morning, our tiny infant would have tubes inserted into a vein in his groin and threaded up into his heart like copper wire in electrical conduit.

There was no question in my mind that the only possible course of action was to pray—to enlist the enormous prayer potential of my family. With my mother doing most of the recruiting, the news was quickly spread to relatives, friends and friends of friends. For when it came to responding to the needs of a community member in trouble, particularly a child, the entire Franco-American community in Lewiston, Maine was basically one gigantic family.

I do believe that the power of prayer not only helped Chad's tiny body keep functioning through his first hospital ordeal, but also guided the hands and minds of the cardiologists who treated him. That prayer energy definitely supported my spirit, preparing me to face whatever I would have to deal with.

I slept hardly at all that night, returning to the hospital early the next morning to face mountains of paperwork. Amos and I were taken to separate rooms and questioned by social workers. Suddenly, our quiet, simple life had been invaded by hordes of strangers, most of whom probably had Chad's welfare in mind, but whose pessimistic attitude made me feel like I should be blaming myself for the defects in Chad's heart. As I completed the endless set of questions, a tiny demon of doubt invaded my thoughts. I remembered taking cold medicines early in my pregnancy so that I could clear my sinuses to sing with my mom's musical group. I'd been pushed to the point where I was considering the possibility that *I* had done this to my son.

After a few minutes of wallowing in guilt, I shook myself out of it, realizing that I needed a clear head for the conversation with Doctor McFaul. It was time to face the results of Chad's cardiac catheterization.

The doctor confirmed and extended his diagnosis. Instead of the normal four valves, Chad's heart had only three, one of them shared by the right and left sides. The left half—usually the stronger pump—was small and weak. Meanwhile, the stronger right half was pumping too much blood into Chad's lungs, more than their blood vessels could handle, with the risk that they would be permanently damaged.

The hole in Chad's heart caused a mixing of blue blood and red blood between its right and left sides. This partially explained his bluish skin color. The right-left imbalance was so great that the flow of blood through Chad's lungs was five times more than through the rest of his body, almost the reverse of normal. Meanwhile, the blood pressure in his body was much too low because of the weakness of his heart's left side.

As if the heart defects weren't enough, Doctor McFaul also told us that there was a kink in Chad's aorta—the main artery of his body.

"What about the drugs?" I asked. "Didn't you say they were helping?"

Doctor McFaul nodded. "We'll continue the Lanoxin to help his heart muscle and add Diuril, a diuretic . . . a type of water pill . . . to prevent fluid buildup in his lungs. It's possible he may do okay, but if not, surgery is indicated to repair his aorta, and reduce the blood flow into his lungs before they sustain irreversible damage."

At the sound of "surgery," Amos and I twitched in unison. The image of our tiny son's chest torn open was gut-wrenching.

Unfortunately, even surgery wasn't really an answer. Doctor McFaul explained that only the aorta and the excessive blood flow to the lungs could be treated. Nothing could be done about the underdeveloped left half of the heart, which would also prevent repairing the hole between the left and right sides.

"The body *does* have incredible healing power," Doctor McFaul said. "Perhaps . . . with time . . . the left side of Chad's heart will grow."

Released from M.M.C. on June 13, 1980, Chad was re-admitted barely a week later. During that period, my small infant continued to struggle for each breath, and God received the prayers of thousands—all offered with the intention that the surgery would be successful.

My prayers went beyond that intention. Who could blame me for wanting a child with a normal heart, a child who could lead a normal life. If the surgeon could repair the problems *outside* Chad's heart, why wasn't it possible for God to do the impossible surgery *inside*. After all, as Jesus had shown in restoring sight to the blind, didn't miracles involve the accomplishment of the humanly impossible?

I met Chad's surgeon, Doctor Nowicki, the evening before the surgery. He seemed too young to shoulder such responsibility.

"Doctor McFaul tells me that you've done this type of surgery on infants several times before," I said.

"Yes, that's true," Doctor Nowicki said. "But each patient is a new challenge, and I always pray for guidance."

"This time you have many people . . . my friends and relatives . . . praying for you," I said.

He smiled, eyelids fluttering. "God has a plan and I know he'll guide my hands so that, hopefully, Chad will get well." He shook my hand. His hands were strong but soft, his grip firm but gentle; like that of a parent guiding his child through traffic on a crowded city street.

In that brief exchange, Doctor Nowicki made me feel

like he recognized God as the healer and himself as an instrument in God's plan.

The following day, as we awaited the results—praying, reading and watching TV to distract ourselves—I began to feel a new strength surging through my mind, another small miracle that I wouldn't immediately recognize because of my preoccupation with larger ones.

Everyone gasped when Doctor McFaul entered from a paneled wooden door at the waiting room's far corner.

"He's out of surgery and recovering in intensive care," Doctor McFaul announced, and the tension in the room released like steam escaping through a check valve. I squeezed Amos's hand and hugged my mom and dad. My sisters, Claire and Ann, and my brother Richard embraced. "Thank God," several voices said.

"Then he's gonna be all right?" my husband asked, hopefully.

"We should see an improvement in his condition," Doctor McFaul said warily. "The surgery to repair the aorta will help blood circulation from his heart to his organs." He held up his hand, thumb and index finger forming a small circle. "And the band placed around his pulmonary artery is controlling the excessive blood flow to his lungs. That's a critical step to prevent lung damage."

As relieved and thankful as I felt, I still wanted more. Like Amos, I wanted Doctor McFaul to answer the question with an unqualified "yes"—no ifs, ands or buts. Down deep, I had a feeling about what might be coming, and I had doubts about my own ability to cope. I glanced over at my mom, one of the strongest people I knew. She had successfully raised seven children over twenty years, yet had suffered through a period when life's pressures had nearly cost her sanity. I wondered if I would be equal to the task of rearing just two children, one of whom had a serious illness. At that moment, I vowed not to give up my quest to find more of God's miraculous grace for my son.

It was not obvious to me at the time, but that grace was already draped around my shoulders. It comforted me the following night, as I rested next to Chad in the Neonatal Intensive Care Unit. I was grateful to be allowed to sleep there, to not be separated from my baby. But sleep didn't come easily. As I watched a small bubble of fluid worm its way up the plastic tube draining fluid from Chad's tiny chest, I distracted myself by focusing on the eerie cat-like cry of an infant across the room, a noise I had almost tuned-out.

Rising from my cot, I wandered over to that other child's crib. For an instant, I stopped breathing, shocked by the baby's appearance. It was hydrocephalic, its head swollen to three times normal size. Its limbs were grotesquely deformed, arms and legs like flippers, with no real fingers or toes.

My heart ached for this poor baby, more for its abandonment than for its deformities. During the two days I spent with Chad in the I.C.U., I did not remember the child receiving even a single visitor except for hospital staff.

Returning to Chad's side until he had fallen asleep, I called for one of the nurses. "Is there any way I can hold him?" I asked, pointing toward the crib of the deformed infant.

The nurse's face lit-up, and she slid a rocking chair toward the crib. "Why don't you sit here, Mrs. Boily, and I'll bring him to you," she said.

As the nurse placed the infant in my arms, he felt incredibly fragile, as if his body had grown so abnormally in the womb that even the muscles and bones refused to stick together. I have never felt a human body so frail. But as I held him against my bosom and rocked him gently, his crying gradually subsided, and his breathing seemed to become calmer.

Thank you, Lord, I thought. *Thank you for giving my son the problems he has, rather than the terrible ones this poor child suffers with. Thank you for my family, and for all the people who pray for and will love Chad no matter how sick he is.*

The hydrocephalic infant fell asleep in my arms.

CHAPTER THREE:
Mining for Miracles

Squirming and tugging at his ear, Chad seemed extremely uncomfortable, so I rose from bed and dragged myself over to his crib. Following a procedure that had already become a reflex by his third month, I carefully felt for a pulse in his neck and positioned my ear close to his face. His heart was beating more than twice each second as it struggled to push enough oxygen around his tiny body.

How can it possibly keep that up? I thought, a knot of fear twisting in my chest. The surgery had kept him alive, but it obviously hadn't been a cure.

His breathing was almost as frantic—one second, one breath—and I listened for any breathing sounds that might alert me to chest congestion. Doctor McFaul had prescribed two different diuretics, but he warned us that any infection— even a simple cold—could trigger fluid buildup in Chad's lungs. What for most children were simple childhood illnesses were for us crises.

Chad continued to squirm and tug at his ear, but I still didn't make the connection between the movements and a simple earache. Preparing myself for a trip to the emergency room, I hurried up to the third floor of our home to make sure my two youngest brothers were all right. They were only a few years older than Amy, and I often took care of them to help out my mom. David and Jim formed a bridge between the two families—at the same time my baby brothers and big brother figures for my children.

"Louise, what's the matter?" David asked.

"I'm worried about Chad. I'm taking him to C.M.M.C.," I said. "Amos will be downstairs if you guys need anything."

"We'll be okay," Jim said. "I just hope Chad is."

Even at eight-years-old, Jimmy's concern for Chad was genuine. Having two such fantastic little brothers made me grateful that my mom's two "mistakes" at the end of her child-bearing years had been born healthy. It seemed to me that there was a message in that situation. My mom and dad had been blessed with seven healthy children; but they had also been faced with huge challenges, raising them on blue-collar incomes and in a house big enough for about half that number. When all nine of us were there together, that house's walls often vibrated, but because of all the love surrounding us, it usually shook with laughter.

It looked like my road was destined to be different from Mom's. Maybe it was my lot to face the challenge of one very ill child, rather than a herd of healthy ones. After all, it was obviously God's will that Chad be born the way he was, and since God loved both my son and myself, there had to be some sense to it all. There just had to be.

♥ ♥ ♥

The emergency room was filled with the usual party-night cases. A burly man who reminded me of my brother, Jerry, sat quietly in a corner, pressing a bloody towel to his mouth. Nearby, a nurse tended to a second man with a gash in his forehead. A teenage couple huddled on the floor, the young boy tightly hugging the shoulders of a blank-faced girl who spastically rocked her head from side to side.

"Come on, Michelle, you're gonna be all right. Just

don't say anything about the blow," I heard the boy say. I was so naive that I thought he was referring to assault rather than to cocaine.

Thank God, infant emergencies were always treated first. After leading me into a cubicle and briefly examining Chad, a nurse returned with an exhausted-looking young doctor, his scrubs spattered with dried blood.

"This child was brought in with otitis, doctor . . . but his respirations are way up," the nurse said to the emergency-room resident. She looked worried.

"He has a heart problem," I said, but neither of them reacted.

The resident clamped the bell of his stethoscope to Chad's chest. "I don't like the sound of this . . . I'm getting a grade-four systolic murmur," he said. He began to draw blood from Chad's tiny foot. "I'm ordering a C.B.C. But make sure the lab knows I want blood gases STAT."

After examining Chad's ear, the doctor turned to leave. "I'm going to find a cardiology resident," he said.

"Oh no, Lord . . . no," I said, convinced that Chad had developed yet another heart-related problem.

"Chad's cardiologist is Doctor McFaul at M.M.C.," I shouted to the resident as he left the room, but he hardly acknowledged my remark.

For over twenty minutes, I waited alone in that room, alternately praying and trying to comfort Chad as he tugged at his ear and occasionally cried out. *What a trooper*, I thought, comparing him to other children with ear infections whom I'd been around. They had screamed endlessly, but my little boy was already showing a courageous tolerance to pain.

Remembering the shock I'd felt when Doctor McFaul had first told us about Chad's heart defects, I braced myself for news about some new complication. By the time the emergency-room resident returned with another young doctor, my back muscles were wound into a hundred little knots.

"Mrs. Boily, this is Doctor Duquette, the cardiology resident," the emergency-room doctor said. I remember thinking that neither man looked any older than me.

Doctor Duquette gently laid his hand on my shoulder. "Mrs. Boily, we're concerned about Chad's low blood oxygen saturation, and we'd like to do some more tests."

Later in Chad's life, I'd develop a pretty fair understanding of blood oxygen saturation and its normal values, but at that moment, all I could think was: *Oh Sweet Jesus, what now*?

"Shouldn't you call Doctor McFaul at M.M.C.?" I said, my voice trembling.

The name had an immediate effect on the young cardiology resident. "How do you know Doctor McFaul?" he asked.

"Like I tried to tell them, he's Chad's cardiologist. My son had surgery at M.M.C. . . . two months ago."

"Excuse me for a moment," the cardiology resident said. He quickly turned and left the examining room. I started praying again.

He returned fifteen minutes later. "I reached Doctor McFaul at home," he said. "He confirmed that at the moment, eighty-eight is a normal value for Chad's blood oxygen saturation."

"What about the sound the other doctor heard—"

"You mean the systolic murmur?" the cardiology resident interrupted. "That's a result of the band surgically placed around Chad's pulmonary artery to reduce blood flow to his lungs. Doctor McFaul confirmed that it's also a normal heart sound for Chad at this point. Nothing to worry about."

"If his heart's okay then you can treat him for the ear

infection," I said, hopefully.

"Not exactly, Mrs. Boily," the resident said. "Because of his heart condition, there's always concern about an infection spreading to his lungs." He pointed toward the hospital exit. "M.M.C. is waiting for you. Would you like me to order an ambulance?"

"Is Chad in any danger?" I asked.

"Right now, his chest is clear," the doctor said.

"Thanks for your help," I said as I collected my things in preparation for the drive from Lewiston to Portland. If an ambulance wasn't absolutely necessary, then we couldn't afford one.

Admitted on August 9, 1980, Chad was discharged two days later, the antibiotic, Amoxicillin added to his list of medications. He had never spiked a fever, and his eating pattern had returned to normal, yet an ear infection—a common childhood problem—had turned into a major scare and a two-day hospital stay.

Two months later, we were back at M.M.C., this time for *two weeks*. It began with a cough and an increase in Chad's already excessive sweating. I rushed him to the pediatrician's office.

"He's breathing even faster than usual, and there appears to be some extra fluid in his left lung," the doctor said after several minutes of listening to Chad's chest with his stethoscope.

"Is his heart failing?" I asked. I had already learned that fluid in the lungs always pointed in that direction.

He shrugged. "He needs to be seen by Doctor McFaul. I'll call down there and set it up. Meanwhile, I'm going to give him a shot of Lasix. It's a stronger diuretic than the ones he's on, and it should help his body get rid of the extra fluid."

Suddenly, we were up to *three* diuretics, and it looked

like Chad's surgery was not making up for the other *un*-repaired problems in his heart. When we arrived in Portland, Doctor McFaul wasted no time in admitting him to M.M.C.

Amos and I spent those two weeks of Chad's hospitalization wondering whether we would ever get to celebrate our son's first birthday. Sometimes, it seemed like his tiny congested lungs were barely able to move thimblefuls of air in and out of his body. *How could he possibly survive, much less ever be normal without enough oxygen*? I obsessed.

Arriving at the hospital toward the end of the first week, I came upon a scene that momentarily stopped my own breathing. The pediatric cardiology unit was a confusion of uniformed bodies-in-motion. I sidestepped a man pushing a silver cart and backed my body against the counter of the nurse's station.

It was another moment before I understood that the flurry of activity indicated an emergency situation in progress. My entire body went limp when I realized that the emergency team was gathering in the room where Chad's crib was located.

Forcing my legs to move, I staggered down that corridor. I don't think I breathed again until I reached the doorway to the room and discovered that it was not my baby the emergency team was treating. But as a nurse eased me away from the scene, I was forced to admit to myself that it could just as easily have been Chad. I knew I had to do something to keep that from happening to us. I had to somehow convince God to keep my son alive.

A few days later, on October 20, Doctor McFaul decided that Chad was well enough to go home. "We're going to keep him on the Lasix and increase his dose of Lanoxin," the doctor told us.

"Then the surgery didn't really help him?" I said,

surprised by my own boldness. It was a question whose answer I was fairly sure I didn't want to hear.

Doctor McFaul held up his hands. "That's not really true, Mrs. Boily . . . it *is* helping to protect his lungs from damage," he said. "The problem is the underdeveloped left side of Chad's heart. I was hoping that it would grow over the months . . . become stronger and work with the surgery to improve his condition—"

"But it hasn't," I said.

Doctor McFaul lowered his eyes slightly. "I'm sorry, but every child born with heart defects is different, and we have no way of anticipating what will occur."

"What about his failure to gain weight?" I asked, concerned that my six-month-old still weighed only about ten pounds.

"That's actually a blessing," Doctor McFaul said. "If he were to grow faster, it would put an additional strain on his heart. It's the fluid accumulation in his lungs we need to be concerned with right now."

I started to walk away.

"Mrs. Boily," Doctor McFaul said. "It's too soon to give up hope that his heart may still get stronger. For the present, we'll do what we can with drug therapy. I'd like to see you again in a week."

Feeling sick to my stomach, I asked my husband to get Chad's things together and told him I'd be right back. I ran down the depressing brown-tiled corridor, took the stairs down to the lobby and burst through the main doors into the cool fall air. The hospital was located on a hill overlooking I-295 and Portland Harbor, and a chilling ocean wind encased my body, carrying me toward a small park behind the medical-center complex. Brushing my long dark hair from my face, I watched the swirling eddies of red, yellow and brown maple leaves forming halos around the dark-green pine branches.

I had always been fascinated by God's plan in making some trees that lost their leaves for the winter, while still leaving us evergreens as a reminder that there was always life, always hope. Although I accepted God's will for us, I refused to give up on the idea that part of his plan might be a miraculous healing for my son. Only God could accomplish what the surgeons couldn't—the healing of the inside of Chad's heart. Perhaps we hadn't prayed hard enough. Maybe our faith wasn't loud enough to reach the ear of God.

At that moment, my mind flashed on the experiences of my youngest sister, Ann, who for several years had been involved in the Catholic Charismatic movement. At that time in Lewiston, the movement was flourishing. Nearly every parish had a Charismatic group, an association of parishioners who frequently came together to pray.

Frantically, I ran back to the main hospital entrance, found a pay phone in the lobby and called my little sister. "Annie, I want you to tell me about some of your experiences with the Charismatics," I said. "I'm thinking of taking Chad there."

"I think it's a great idea," Ann said.

"What'll it be like?" I asked.

"They'll probably surround you and Chad and focus their prayer energy into you," she said. "Sometimes, I've seen the person who's prayed-over slain in the spirit."

"What do you mean, 'slain in the spirit'?"

"They sort of collapse and go unconscious, but fall like a feather into the arms of group members," Ann explained. "When they come around, they always feel better . . . refreshed, more hopeful."

Ann also described how members of the group would sometimes speak in tongues, a phenomenon described in the Bible. Ann herself had experienced it.

"What's it feel like?" I asked.

"Like you're filled with God's grace, and the Holy Spirit is declaring its presence," Ann said. "Like everything you say has meaning for everybody . . . because it's God's word . . . spoken through you."

As I climbed the stairway to Chad's room to bring my son home from his two weeks at M.M.C., I vowed that I would ask the Charismatics for help. We needed some kind of miracle.

♥ ♥ ♥

For a while, my sister, Claire and I attended the meeting of a small Charismatic group. Gathered in a single room, the community would read the Bible aloud and listen to members preach about the power and love of God. Claire and I prayed intensely for healing.

During the next few months, my two sisters and I attended the prayer meetings of a larger Charismatic group recommended by a friend of my mother's. I distinctly remember the first night we went there, because at the top of the house's walkway, an elderly man accosted us. He was knurled and hunched-over, and he seemed to materialize from the shadows as though he had been part of them. He intercepted us before we could ring the doorbell.

"Don't enter this house of blasphemy," the old man growled.

My sister Ann boldly stepped forward and spoke in angry tones that I didn't think her capable of: "Good Christian people live here. How can you say that?"

"Because I've been here . . . many times," the old man said. "I have heard how they babble the devil's tongue. Black magic."

"The Bible says that speaking in tongues is a gift from

the Holy Spirit," Ann argued. "I've experienced it, myself. It's a wonderful feeling."

His face contorting in anger, the old man shouted at my little sister: "Then *you* are also a blasphemer."

As I turned my body to shield Chad from the cold November wind, my sister Claire stepped between Ann and the old man. "How dare you say that to my sister," Claire said. "Get away from us."

"Please . . . I'm just here to ask God's help for my sick child," I begged. "He's only a baby."

The old man took a step back and clutched at his chest. "I found no healing here," he said.

"You have to have faith before God can heal you," Claire said.

"There is no God in this house," the man insisted.

Ann rang the doorbell. "You need to find God in your heart. But yours is full of hate," she said.

He stepped forward and gestured toward the front door. "Yes, I *hate* those who promise what they can't deliver."

Thankfully, the door opened and Ann pulled me in. Still facing the old man, Claire backed through the door after us. "Go away and leave us alone," she said, harshly.

"Remember . . . I gave you fair warning. There is no healing here," the man said, as the door closed.

I was shaken-up by the encounter. At the time, I tried to brush it off, so I could concentrate on the reason we had come. But thinking back, I have to wonder whether that old man wasn't an obstacle put in my path to test my faith. I've sometimes even wondered whether he was real. Maybe he was a spirit, a shadowy reflection of a weakness in my trust in God.

The house was swarming with people, and after opening prayers, I was asked to stand at the center of the largest room, where a tight circle formed around me with each person touching me. Around that inner circle gathered larger circles, each member laying hands on someone in the circle closer to me.

"Praise be to God for healing Chad Boily's heart," they prayed, and even though I was never *slain in the spirit*, I felt wonderful warmth radiating though my body. Maybe it was just an emotional vibration coming from the caring energy of so many people who seemed to genuinely want to see our ordeal end. But whatever it was, I left each of those meetings with renewed hope and a more positive outlook.

As tempted as I was to believe that Chad's heart would be healed, I also understood that it would be a huge miracle. I believed in miracles, and I imagined the confused doctors staring at an X-ray, then telling us that all the heart defects had disappeared. But I also realized that no one could possibly understand the mind of God. Ann reminded me that during her many years with the Charismatics, she'd observed that healings often came in a back-door way rather than exactly how they were asked for. *Let go, let God*, I thought, remembering the phrase from an A.A. member I knew.

There is no doubt in my mind that at a spiritual and maybe even at a physical level, a healing *did* occur during that period. Chad's next few cardiac catheterizations showed no real change in the size of his weak heart and no closure of the hole inside. But Chad refused to fade away, and both his pediatricians and Doctor McFaul were amazed that he did so well under the circumstances.

Just after Chad's second birthday, in May of 1982, Doctor McFaul spoke with us about the results of a catheterization he had just performed.

"The data shows that Chad's heart is functioning better than most of us had hoped," the doctor said. "Frankly, we anticipated that his shared valve would have developed leakage by now, but it hasn't. And somehow, with the help of the drugs, his weak left side manages to circulate enough blood to keep him going."

"Do you know why?" I asked.

"I have to plead a certain level of ignorance, Mrs. Boily," he said sheepishly. "But I'm also flexible enough to graciously accept positive news . . . even when I don't completely understand it."

Although blueness would return to Chad's skin if he exerted himself, his color stayed fairly normal when he rested. It was like the invisible hand of a guardian angel enclosed his left ventricle, helping it squeeze with each heartbeat. In Doctor McFaul's written report, he evaluated Chad's heart function as "quite satisfactory."

More important, as Chad got older, he showed us a terrific attitude, which was as significant as any medical test result. Chad just never thought of himself as sick. I watched gratefully as he learned to walk and talk right on schedule, thankful that my son appeared to be blessed with a normal brain.

I began to feel less fragile about him, more inclined to leave him with my parents for a few hours at their lakeside camp. And time after time, when I'd return to pick him up, my mother would give me a positive report on her grandson's condition.

"How's Chad, Mom?" I would ask immediately.

"He must be okay, Louise," my mother would answer, smiling. "Every time I ask him how he's feeling, he always tells me: 'I'm fine Memé; I feel fine.' "

CHAPTER FOUR:
The Loner

I recall the time around my little brother's birth as a bewildering jumble of joy, tearful sadness and prayer. At just four-years-old, I was incapable of interpreting the significance of the confusion surrounding me.

From that first month of Chad's life, my mother did her best to shield me from the severity of his illness. She never administered Chad's medications in my presence. And I'm sure that she must have given the family strict orders to exclude me from discussions about my brother's health. Mom wanted me to have a normal childhood, unblemished by her preoccupation with Chad's condition.

"When's Mom coming home, Memé?" I'd ask my grandmother on any of the numerous occasions that Chad was hospitalized over those first two years.

"She has to stay with Chad tonight in the hospital," my grandmother would reply.

"Chad's sick again?"

She would smile broadly. "Yes, but don't you worry, Amy, he's getting better and he'll be home soon."

Regardless of who was taking care of me—my grandparents, my aunt or a friend—I was always presented with smiling faces and upbeat attitudes about my brother's prognosis.

Yet when I peek back through that veil of optimism, I also recall incidents that, had I been less naive and less vigorously reassured, would have led my mind in quite a different direction.

I remember overhearing my mom and my grandmother talking about "buying time," referring to the fact that Chad's physicians were essentially doing their best to keep him alive until some new procedure came along that they could use on his heart. As a current student of medical science, I now understand why the extent of the defects in Chad's heart gave some of those physicians reason to wonder whether he would survive much beyond his sixth birthday.

Perhaps it was her fear of losing Chad that prompted Mom to turn my attention away from illness. I believe she was also striving to create an environment in which her two children could form the special bond between brother and sister, a unique type of love that she herself had experienced within her close-knit family.

What predominates in my recollections of those elementary-school years is an image of the little brother with a great attitude, who loved to smile and was even fonder of drawing smiles from others. Chad naturally attracted attention as much because of his magnetic personality as because of the curiosity factor entailed in his illness.

I loved my brother dearly, and I don't recall feeling jealous or resentful because of the spotlight focused on him. Ironically, it was only the inquiries of adults that pushed my mind in an unhealthy direction.

"How does it feel when your brother gets all the attention and you don't?" I'd be asked; or, even worse: "What does it feel like to be the first grandchild, but the one that's pushed aside?"

I would shrug and shake my head. "I never feel like that," I'd answer honestly.

As I got older, those ongoing questions became a mini-course in perverse psychology. Ultimately, as I approached my teens, they would impress upon me an awareness that childhood ingenuousness is a wonderful thing, until it's subjected to the distorted misconceptions of certain adults—people who have, unfortunately, lost their connection with that untainted innocence.

The endless suggestions that I was the "lesser child" must have eventually wormed their way into my emotions, for I do recall one incident when I questioned the equality with which my mother dispensed affection.

I was almost eight years old and was amusing myself on the swing set in our back yard. Since Chad was also on the swings, Mom was outside as well. He was so frail that she never felt she could risk leaving him alone in that situation. And to her credit, Mom recognized that I was still too young to saddle with such a large responsibility.

Trying to slow down my swing, I caught the toe of my shoe in a rut in the dirt and fell off. Although I wasn't really hurt, I started bawling—an almost operatic performance of anguish.

"Amy, come on, now, you're not hurt . . . you just fell off the swing," Mom said encouragingly. "That's my big girl . . . you're going to be fine . . . see." She gently brushed the dirt off my leg.

As I stopped crying, Chad toddled over to the seesaw, climbed on and immediately fell off. Perhaps emulating his big sister, he began to wail and holler, immediately drawing Mom's attention.

Mom ran over to him, scooped him off the ground and cradled him as though he were a fragile porcelain doll. "Oh Chad, you poor thing," she said, kissing his face, arms and hands.

I looked at my mother with tears welling-up in my eyes again. "Mom, does this mean I'm too old to get kisses and hugs like Chad?" I asked.

Mom gently set Chad on the lawn, then encased me in a warm hug. "Of course not," she said, "you're never too old for kisses and hugs."

Years later, my mother would tell me about the lesson I had taught her that day. She became even more aware of those special times when her daughter needed some extra nurturing, be it a smile, a hug or a mother-to-daughter conversation over lunch. As she herself grew in parental sagacity, my mother learned that the difficulty of rearing a healthy child in the shadow of a mortally ill one was an inescapable part of the overall challenge that God had presented her. Mom became a continual learner, growing constantly in her understanding of interpersonal dynamics. If there were colleges that offered degrees predicated on life experience, she would certainly qualify for a Ph.D. in practical family sociology.

Mom's talents also extended into the realm of low-budget interior decorating. We lived on the second and third floors of a house that was artfully embellished by virtue of her skill with sewing machine, paintbrush and even plaster trowel. She could turn pennies into luxurious looking highlights. Yet, despite all the care and hard work that she invested in its appearance, she never prohibited us from playing anywhere in the house.

Some of my earliest recollections are of myself and Chad playing indoor hide-and-seek with our "big-brothers," Uncles Jim and David. Invariably, Chad and I would rush to hide behind a couch in the corner of the living room. Chad's diminutive size made it easy for him to rapidly squeeze his body into the space, while I had a much tougher time of it.

"Move over, Chad," I'd whisper.

"Can't . . . no more room," he'd answer nonchalantly.

Typically, Jim would finish his count, "eighty-five . . .

ninety . . . ninety-five . . . a hundred," while I was still struggling to lower my head and shoulders out of sight.

"I see Amy, one-two-three . . . behind the couch," Jim would shout, spotting the top of my wavy light-brown mane.

Despite his well-hidden position, Chad's discovery would usually occur immediately after mine, since my inability to escape detection would always send him into uncontrolled spasms of laughter.

I don't ever remember him struggling for breath during or after one of those good cackles. It was as though the laughter bubbling through his body acted as a supplement to raise the oxygen saturation of his blood above what his weak heart and lungs could accomplish alone. Sometimes, I imagined that Chad had a perpetually giddy guardian angel to whom God had given the assignment of making sure to set Chad's attitude for the day by thoroughly tickling him every morning.

Unfortunately, breathing did not come as easily to my brother when he tried to play with other boys his age. Because of his positive attitude, he readily attracted other children to himself. But the moment he engaged in any game that required continuous exertion—kick ball, street hockey, or basketball—he would rapidly become so short of breath, that even continuing to stand was a genuine struggle.

It was the only situation during which I remember him complaining about his health. "Amy, I can't breath . . . can't breathe," he said, lips turning purple.

I knelt beside my brother and put my arm around him. "Come on, Chad, you better go upstairs and rest," I said, echoing words I'd heard so often from my mother.

"But I wanna play," Chad insisted.

"Look at him, he's turnin' purple," one of his playmates pointed out.

"Purple, purple, eueuuwww," a second boy mocked.

"His heart's sick. He was born that way . . . it's not his fault," I tried to explain.

But the first little boy would not be moved to sympathy. "My dad says to stay away from him; says he's gonna die," he brashly declared.

"Dieyi, dieyi; he's gonna dieyi," the other boy ridiculed.

"You shut up. He is not," I said. I shoved the little boy to the ground and stood menacingly between him and my brother.

"You pushed me; I'm tellin'," he said, looking up from his seat on the sidewalk.

"So see if I care," I said, trying to be nonchalant, even though I was concerned that his parents might make trouble for me.

"Is too gonna die . . . is too," the first boy persisted. He spat at Chad.

I couldn't contain my anger. I threw a roundhouse punch and connected on his arm.

"You get out of here," I yelled, shaking my fist at the both of them. I helped Chad to his feet and led him toward the rear door of our house.

"You hit me; I'm tellin' my mother," the boy said.

I called back over my shoulder: "So tell her . . . you little jerk. Next time you spit at my brother, I'll hit you harder."

The explosive anger and the violence were totally out of character for me. But those kids pushed my buttons like nothing else I recall from my childhood. For several years, I think I subliminally believed that children inherently possessed a streak of malevolence. It took me a while to realize that it was really an expression of parental prejudice.

It was bad enough that in Lewiston, Maine, a boy's stature—and with it, his self-image—was largely determined either by his athletic prowess or by how tough he was with his fists. In Chad's case, the situation was compounded by family history. Our dad had been one of the all-time-great soccer stars at Lewiston's Saint Dominic's High School, from which our mom and all of her brothers and sisters would ultimately graduate. Meanwhile with his lack of stamina, Chad could never play any sport long enough to learn it well, much less master it. It has always bothered me that those little boys who mocked Chad never appreciated how tough my little brother really was.

My mother was aware of the situation, and she did everything in her power to encourage Chad's friendships with boys his own age. In the winter, she'd open up our house and invite Chad's elementary school classmates for sleepovers, driving all around the city to pick them up when their parents couldn't or wouldn't transport them.

Mom also sent both of us to summer day camp for a few years, probably because she thought it might help Chad make friends while I was there to keep an eye on him. But day camp turned out to be a repeat performance for my brother. The boys Chad's own age spent much of their time at swimming, diving and all the other aerobic water sports that Chad's weak heart just couldn't sustain.

Unable to participate in diving and swimming contests, Chad became even more of a loner, going off to amuse himself with odd-shaped or interestingly colored rocks, small animals of any variety, or anything else that his increasingly fertile imagination became intrigued with. I did my best to include him in my activities with my own friends, but I soon discovered that a six-year-old boy wasn't thrilled with sandcastle contests or most other ten-year-old-girl projects.

Chad basically adopted the attitude that if no one else was going to do anything of interest with him, then he would have to do it on his own. It was during that period when he was first attracted to magic. He would read, watch television shows and practice with whatever materials he could get hold of. And the more he practiced, the better his skills became.

There were three aspects to magic that more generally reflected the personality characteristics that sustained Chad in his isolation. First, magic was something that required ingenuity, that involved experimentation to figure out how things were done; second, it was something he could master—be better at than most people around him; third, and most important, it was a way to elicit a reaction from others. As he got older, Chad would sometimes go to extremes to achieve that end.

His early attempts at creating illusion were primitive and showed a disposition toward the grisly. It started with his severed-fingertip-in-a-box illusion. He cut a hole in the bottom of a small cardboard box filled with cotton. Then, after saturating the cotton with red food coloring, he would insert his finger into the hole and through the cotton, so that only the fingertip was visible. He'd then parade around the house, proudly exhibiting what he claimed was his severed fingertip.

As the detail with which Chad perpetrated his illusions improved, they sometimes succeeded in suckering Mom because of her ongoing anxiety about his health. For example, there was the time he used rubber cement to glue a rubber finger onto his hand at an angle which made it appear that one of his own fingers had been snapped backward and broken. To achieve a more realistic-looking fake blood, he used red food coloring thickened with cornstarch. For fractured bone, he carved a small shard of balsa wood into what he envisioned as the shape of a shattered finger bone and positioned it so that it prominently protruded from the "bleeding, dislocated" rubber finger.

"Mom, Amy, I caught my finger in the door and it's really in bad shape," he said, running into my room and unveiling it from beneath a crimson-stained towel with the style and panache of an accomplished magician.

Mom dropped the sewing needle she was using to baste a hem on one of my skirts. She covered her mouth with her hand as though on the verge of vomiting. "Oh my God, Chad, oh my God."

She jumped up and ran toward the kitchen. "Amy, call nine-one-one. I'm going to try . . . to stop the bleeding," she called behind her.

Luckily, I spotted the stringy residue of rubber cement and realized that it was only one of Chad's more lurid tricks.

"Mom, it's just one of Chad's crazy magic tricks," I called out. At least it saved Mom the embarrassment of having to explain the false alarm to emergency medical services.

"You're a jerk, Chad Boily," I said to my brother.

"It's what?" my mother shrieked as she reappeared at my bedroom doorway.

Chad smiled, held up his hand, and pulled off the rubber finger. "Pretty good one, huh Mom?" he said.

Mom waved her fist at him. "Yeah, good for nothing. Don't you ever scare me like that again, Chad."

Her warning never really did deter Chad from honing his black art. He continued to improve his ability to present such convincing illusions that he was finally able to count me among the beguiled.

One evening, as I was sitting at the kitchen table doing my homework, I heard what sounded like Chad's voice calling from his room. It was loud but muffled, as though either his throat was sore or there was something blocking his mouth.

It definitely sounded different from his normal pre-bedtime banter, which generally accompanied his donning Superman or Aquaman pajamas and pretending to rescue damsels-in-distress. Tonight, there was no monologue of bravado from our bedroom superhero, only what sounded like cries of distress.

"Mom, Amy, come quick," he called out. "Help . . . I'm not sure I wanna do this."

Bolting from her bedroom, my mother sprinted down the short hallway to the kitchen, nearly knocking me from my chair as she turned the corner into the living room. At the room's far end, she threw open the door to Chad's room and emitted a bone-jarring scream. Right behind, I pushed past her into Chad's small bedroom.

For an instant, I stopped breathing and my knees buckled. Noose around his neck, Chad hung from the ceiling— nearly ten feet in the air—just over the edge of his loft bed. His breathing was labored, and he grunted, as though he was choking.

Since his skin color never looked very healthy anyway, it was hard to tell exactly how bad his condition really was. My mother and I stood there, shocked and terrified, unable to move.

Suddenly a huge smile blossomed across Chad's face. "Gotcha," he said, laughing and clapping his hands.

I started breathing in short shallow bursts, my own gasps eerily in synch with the rhythm of my brother's macabre laughter.

My mother lurched forward. "Chad Boily, you scared me half to death," she said. "No wonder I have gray hairs already."

"Aw Mom, it's just a trick," Chad said, his laughter curtailed slightly by Mom's anger.

This time, Chad's imagination had gotten the best of both of us. Captivated by his ingenuity, I climbed half way up the ladder to his loft bed. Somehow, he had managed to affix a lightly colored cloth belt to the corner post of the loft, looping it under his arms to support his body in mid-air and making it appear that he was actually hanging by the neck from a realistic-looking noose that he'd fashioned from clothesline.

As Mom's anger melted into relief, Chad freed himself from his cincture and climbed down from the loft to give her a hug. "You gotta admit, it was a great trick, Mom," he said.

"Yeah . . . great . . . in five minutes, it took five years off my life," Mom said, hugging him like she would never ever let him go. It was one of those moments that reaffirmed my mother's determination to do anything to keep Chad with us.

♥ ♥ ♥

About that time in our lives, I first began to really notice my father's absence. He would often come home late, and lying in bed, I'd be awakened by the sound of angry voices. At first I thought that my parents were arguing over my dad's cigarette habit. Chad and I became Mom's allies in the quest to get Dad to quit smoking, because we loved him and didn't want to see him hurt himself.

After a while, I realized that the arguments went beyond just cigarettes, extending to my father's abuse of alcohol. I remember one instance when Dad arrived home early, before Mom had tucked Chad and me in for the night. From the look on my brother's face, I could tell that he realized, as I did, that Dad had been drinking.

The pattern continued more-or-less unabated, and as my hostility toward my father grew, I couldn't understand how Chad maintained his positive attitude. In retrospect, I realize that his reaction to the situation was forged from the basic personality traits that always carried Chad through: love, acceptance and honesty. Chad's love was so strong that he would sometimes hide my father's cigarettes in a futile attempt to stop him from smoking. And ultimately, he could accept and forgive Dad for everything—everything but the deceitfulness.

One morning, after my parents had engaged in a particularly acerbic argument the prior night, I overheard a conversation between my father and brother.

"Dad, I heard you and Mom yelling again last night," Chad said.

"Don't worry about it, Chad; your mom was just mad that I got home late," my father said.

"Dad, I don't want you to get sick from the cigarettes," Chad said, softly.

"I'm not doing that anymore, Chad."

To my surprise, I heard my six-year-old brother raise his voice over his normally subdued monotone: "Don't try to fool me, Dad. Don't tell me you don't. I can smell it. It hurts me when you tell me you don't do that, because I know you do."

I was stunned, and my father was speechless. My kindhearted little brother had done something of great courage, something my own anger made me incapable of. He had said it like it was, expressed his hurt, yet had delivered the message on an undertone of love rather than one of malice. It was the type of interaction that made it impossible for my father to ignore the fact that his diminutive son with the damaged heart loved him ten normal hearts' worth. The incident represented one of the first concrete blocks in a new foundation that would ultimately enable both of them to sustain a mutual love through all that was yet to come.

♥ ♥ ♥

It seemed like there were always solutions to problems lurking somewhere in Mom's large family. At a time in his life when Chad lacked both friends and a close paternal relationship, my uncles and my grandfather were there to help fill those voids.

David and Jim would do anything to make Chad laugh, and in the process, devised ways to fulfill Chad's need to be a boy without overtaxing his heart. Chad loved to watch the two of them wrestle, and afterward, he would taunt them with a challenge.

"I can take you guys," he'd say. "Come on, hit me." He would offer his arm.

"Okay, you're on, chump," one of my uncles would say, and lightly tap Chad on the shoulder.

Stepping forward, Chad would punch his adversary on the arm or chest. Legs collapsing, the punch's recipient would fall to the floor, while the other one immediately lined up for his turn to do combat with my brother. The harder and more frequently they fell, the harder Chad laughed. It got to the point where Jimmy's first act when he came over for a visit was to spontaneously collapse into a heap on our kitchen floor. My uncles just couldn't get enough of Chad's laughter, and there was something about the ersatz boxing matches that satisfied Chad's deep need for male companionship and male-centered activity. In their own intuitive way, my two uncles, themselves barely teenagers, were board-certified psychologists where their nephew was concerned.

Both excellent athletes, Dave and Jim also tried to include Chad in toned-down sports activities other than mock boxing. But they quickly realized that my brother's weak heart precluded even the mildest exertion.

One day, as they kicked at a soccer ball on the lawn in front of my grandparents' camp, my mom pulled her youngest brother aside and issued a warning that Jimmy heard but never completely accepted: "Jim, you've got to realize that Chad is crippled because of his heart."

Jim looked stunned. Out of respect for his eldest sister, he made no reply. Instead, after my mother had walked away, he turned to me and in a half-whisper, declared what he'd wanted to shout at my mom: "Amy, I'll *never* think of Chad as a cripple. *Never*."

It was part anger, part unconscious prayer. Like the perfect big brother figure, Jim wanted badly to teach Chad to play the sports that he was so adept at—particularly soccer and hockey. And he refused to give up hope that Chad's health would someday improve, that he would someday be able to run and skate without succumbing to complete breathlessness.

But a belief in miracles did not stop my uncles from behaving as pragmatists in the interim. After conferring for several moments, they decided that for the present, Chad would have to be taught low-exertion, non-contact sports. David and Jim led Chad to a small inlet of the lake just down the dirt road from the camp.

Affectionately known as the "frog pond," the little pool provided the perfect habitat for amphibian feeding and reproduction, and especially in springtime, it harbored everything from tadpoles to bullfrogs. At first, Dave and Jim gave Chad a net to work with, but within minutes, my brother was closely observing their technique for barehanded frog trapping.

"See, it's easy, buddy . . . as long as you move slow until you're right over them with the net. Then you trap 'em quick," David said.

"Go 'head, Chad try it," Jimmy encouraged.

Chad dropped the net at the shore of the pond and waded in, planting his feet and sinking down into the muck at the pond's bottom.

"What're you doing, Chad? Use the net, it's easier," David said.

"Don't need no net," Chad insisted.

Suddenly, Chad leaned forward, extended his hands and plucked a small frog from the pond on his first try.

"All right, Chad," David hooted.

Jimmy shook his head and smiled. "Unbelievable," he said. "Unbelievable."

A few minutes later, Chad had trapped his first big one, a huge, slimy bullfrog with a yellow underbelly. His face glowing with the thrill of accomplishment, Chad tucked the animal securely into a red plastic pail and started up the dirt road toward camp. When he arrived, he found a large ready-made audience. In addition to the normal throng of aunts, uncles and friends often found at camp, this happened to be a day when several of my grandmother's sisters—our great aunts—were visiting, including Aunt Simone, the wonderful woman who had been Mom's support during those first revelations about Chad's heart defects.

Even at his young age, Chad recognized the extrovert of the group, the person from whom he could elicit the largest reaction. Cupping his little hands around the bullfrog, he lifted it from the plastic pail. "*Ma tante* Simone, look what I caught," he said.

As Simone leaned over, Chad thrust the bullfrog, yellow belly up, within inches of her face.

Simone froze for a moment, believing that it was a plastic toy. But when the creature suddenly extended a sizable leg that barely missed oozing slime on her face, Simone jumped back.

Her face twisted into a look of half-surprise, half-revulsion. "Oh my goodness, Chad, where did you get that ugly thing?" she said before relieving her shock with a fit of good-natured laughter.

From that moment on, Chad quickly became the acknowledged expert-level frog-catcher, able to outstrip anyone in spotting and bare-handing them. During early evenings at camp, I would frequently hear my mother's voice calling my brother's name off in the distance. As the sun approached the ridge across the lake, and the familiar odor of hot dogs and burgers searing on my grandfather's gas grill signaled that dinner was imminent, Chad could be found literally knee-deep in the muck at the frog pond's bottom, scouring the surroundings for frogs, turtles and the occasional snake.

"Chad get out of that mud . . . there's blood suckers down there," Mom would warn. "Besides, it's time for dinner."

"Aw Mom, I don't care about any blood suckers," he would complain softly before emerging from the ooze like some revivified prehistoric anthropoid, snails crawling on his feet, pond grass dragging behind him.

"Look at this one, Mom. Got seven today." He held up his latest catch.

"That's a nice one, honey. I hope you didn't find any snakes. You know how Memé hates them."

"Nah, but I can find one tomorrow." He flashed Mom the impish grin that signified the special bond between them. It wasn't that Mom had any particular affection for frogs, but she understood that they represented something special to Chad.

Besides the fact that it probably helped him learn how to count and add, frog catching was "boy stuff," a physical accomplishment that Chad had learned to do better than his two athlete uncles—indeed, better than anyone else. I think it brought him an enormous satisfaction that only someone in his position could fully appreciate. As usual, family members picked up on it as an activity that brightened Chad's spirit, that invariably brought a smile to his face, and so almost everyone encouraged it. Chad's smiles were everyone's smiles.

There was never any cruelty involved. After observing and petting the frog for a few minutes, Chad would release the animal into the shallow water near the boat dock and watch its movements for a few minutes, confident that he'd someday meet up with it again back at the frog pond.

It was that same boat dock from which Chad would frequently fish for the few bass left in the lake. Besides being a low-exertion sport, fishing also offered many male role models including my father, and Mom's brothers: Jerry, Richard, David and Jim. It was another sport that didn't stress Chad's heart and that involved animals.

One of Chad's best fishing buddies was our grandfather, Pepère Bob. Pepé would often sit with Chad for hours, explaining fishing techniques, or being there to help when my brother had trouble securing a lure or freeing a yellow perch from his hook. Of the many men in my family who did their utmost to enrich my brother's life, my grandfather deserves a special place for his patience and consistency.

Frog catching and fishing weren't the only "boy stuff" that Chad shared with his male relations. He quickly showed a penchant for off-color humor as well. For example, as is sometimes the case among American men, farting was elevated to the status of competitive sport among the males in my family. It began with Chad's joining in with the laughter that often accompanied a loudly reported burst of gas, the guffawing especially vigorous if one of the women in the family criticized the tactlessness of the practice.

"You guys are so gross," my mom or one of my aunts

would object.

"I can't believe you don't appreciate what a good one that was," the windbreaker would retort.

"Why don't you take it outside and away from mixed company and let us breathe in here."

Because of his fondness for eliciting reactions, the next step was to become a participant in the games, and Chad often tried to match his uncles fart for fart. In turn, reinforced by Chad's positive emotional reaction to the "game," several formalities were incorporated, including the finger-pulling, gas-pressure-release trigger mechanism.

"Jimmy, pull my finger," Chad would often exclaim as Jim reached the top of the stairs leading up to our apartment. Over time, the greeting spread to other male family members, who by either reputation or action, identified themselves to my brother as being members of the gassers club.

Nor was this the only strange custom that developed between Chad and Jim. My uncle spent so much time with us that he often slept over, and the extra bed on the third floor more-or-less became Jimmy's. But Jimmy's "bedroom" was actually an oversized dormer off the third-floor's main room, a recreation room with a pool table where my father taught Chad to play the game. The ceilings were peaked— following the roofline—and in the dormer, Jimmy's bed was tucked under a ceiling that allowed him barely a foot of space over his sleeping body.

On any morning when Jim slept over, you'd be likely to find Chad creeping up the orange-carpeted stairs to the third floor before anyone else was about. At the top, he would crawl across the main room, silently enter the dormer and slither over to the head of Jimmy's bed.

"Jimmy, wake up," I would hear him yell, followed by a loud thud like the sound of a large rock dropped onto a sidewalk. For the next several seconds, the sounds of Chad's uproarious laughter would predominate. Jimmy was such a good sport that he'd join in the merriment within seconds—despite the aching in his head.

Sometimes it seemed like the two of them would find a reason to laugh even if the nightly news were to announce the impending Apocalypse. There is no doubt in my mind that after family prayer, it was that familial laughter that did the most to bolster my brother's weak heart during those years when no cardiologist could find any convincing medical reason for his ongoing sustenance.

CHAPTER FIVE:
New Beginnings

*T*oward the end of the 80's, I became complacent about Chad's condition. I, of course, realized that his heart was still deformed, but I let myself believe that through the grace of God, he would continue to survive with that heart. I suppose I was in denial, but for eight years I had struggled against the thought that I was bound to someday see my son's face on an obituary page. I was desperate to be free of those terrible fears.

Perhaps it was also the shaky feeling associated with the disintegration of my marriage that distracted me. Or maybe it was the shock of turning thirty; or my new job as a teacher's aide for special-needs children. Whatever the case, a routine visit to M.M.C. in the spring of 1988 snapped me back to reality.

As he emerged from the examining room, Doctor McFaul gently pointed me to a chair near his desk. "How long has Chad shown the increased cyanosis . . . blueness in his skin, Mrs. Boily?"

I gasped. "Blueness! I hadn't really noticed any difference."

"What about his energy level?"

I shook my head. "It hasn't been very good . . . but then he hasn't been himself. He's been depressed about my separation from his father."

"I'd like you to watch him closely between now and

your next visit—"

"Oh Lord, doctor, is he getting sick again?"

Doctor McFaul sidestepped the question. "I'd like to know if he tires more easily. It may be time to consider the procedure I had mentioned to you."

My guts twisted. The procedure was a type of experimental heart surgery called the "Fontan Method," which up to that moment, Doctor McFaul had always been hesitant about. He had warned us that the European surgeons doing the operation were not having completely positive results. In retrospect, I can see that Doctor McFaul knew Chad would eventually need to undergo surgery. But years before, in a letter to Chad's pediatrician, he had described that operation as having a "very, very high rate of mortality." As a result, I had written it off as a treatment I would only agree to in a life-threatening emergency.

On the flip side, 1988 brought us the best neighbors life could offer. With her husband, Bob in medical school, my sister, Claire had moved her family and their trailer just next door onto an extra piece of land we owned. As my marriage continued to deteriorate, Claire became an even more important support for me, and her young twin daughters an outlet for Chad's affection.

As hard as I tried to encourage friendships with boys his own age, there was only so much I could do to break down their barriers of fear and mistrust about Chad's illness. Maybe those kids didn't know any better, but their rejection was very damaging to Chad's self-image, especially when they excluded him from activities in which he was perfectly able to participate. I never did understand it.

For instance, one day, my brother Jim swung by Chad's school to pick him up, only to find Chad standing at the edge of a group of children conversing near the schoolyard fence. A night at the movies was being planned, and Jim recognized most of the kids from around the neighborhood. He couldn't help listening in from his car.

"You comin', Lou?" a boy named Skip asked.

"Yeah, what's playin'?" Lou answered.

"*RoboCop*. Ricky Michaud said it's the coolest movie he's seen in two years. Outrageous special effects."

"How we gonna get in? Couldn't see it last year 'cause my dad wouldn't take me," Lou said.

"That's what's so cool," Skip said. "Now that my sister's workin' there, we don't need no adults."

"Outrageous. Count me in," Lou said.

"I wanna come too," a girl at the edge of the group complained.

"This ain't no girls' movie," Lou argued.

Skip, the organizer, overruled his friend. "She can come if she brings somethin' to eat."

"I'll bring brownies," the girl volunteered.

Jim watched Chad push toward the center of the group, hoping to be noticed. "I can bring candy . . . or whatever," Chad offered.

Not only did everyone ignore Chad, but instead of answering him, Skip pointed at a boy standing right next to him. "You comin' Joey?" Skip asked.

"Don't got no money," Joey said.

In a last-ditch effort for recognition, Chad pulled several dollars from his pocket. "I got some money," he said, holding up the cash.

Joey snatched the bills from Chad's hand. "Great, I'll pay you back . . . whenever," he said.

Floored by the backfiring of his ploy to be acknowledged, Chad backed his way out of the group toward the schoolyard gate, his eyes filling with tears.

Jimmy got out of his car and threw an arm around Chad's shoulder. "C'mon buddy, you don't need these bozos.

Let's go home. We'll rent a video tonight . . . on me."

Everyone in the group had been invited to go—except Chad. My brother Jim found it hard to believe that anyone, even eight-year-olds, could be so insensitive.

At other times, when Chad *was* included, plans would sometimes suddenly change, and everyone but Chad would be notified. I remember how depressed he looked after he returned from one of those group outings.

"That must've been a short movie, Chad," I said.

"Anybody call me on the phone, Mom?"

I shook my head. "No, honey; why?"

"Didn't see any movie, Mom."

"How come?"

He shrugged. "Nobody else showed up."

Characteristically, Chad turned some of that frustration into positive energy. He took great pleasure in spending time with his cousins, Sarah and Christine, and he would do most anything to make them laugh. From pushing their swings, to making chocolate sundaes in his mouth, to flopping on the ground just as his uncles had done to amuse him, Chad never let his own bad treatment sour his basic affection for people.

That affection often translated into a desire to help, to do a good deed for someone, especially someone in his family. Imagine my surprise when my young son complained that I never let him help change his year-old cousins' diapers when I was babysitting for Claire. I recall the time when he took it upon himself to do so—first one twin, then the other— in each case, doing a perfect job.

Not that Chad didn't have his foolish moments; and some of those moments were definitely connected to his need to be recognized by boys his own age. One incident in particular sticks out in my mind.

In preparation for entering high school, Amy was asked

to obtain parental permission to participate in a sex-education class. Because she seemed so nervous about it, I decided to give her a mini-course, the night before the actual class, and I asked my new friend, Brian for help. As part of the presentation, Brian unpackaged several condoms and explained their use as both contraceptives and protectors against sexually transmitted diseases.

Suddenly, we heard a shuffling sound on the stairway to the third floor. Chad was eavesdropping on the sex-ed mini-course.

"By fitting over the man's penis, they serve two functions," Brian explained to Amy. "First, they protect him from getting any infections that the woman may have . . . or passing on ones that he might have."

"Like AIDS?" Amy asked.

Brian nodded. "That's right. Second, they prevent his sperm from reaching the woman's egg. But they don't always work perfectly as a method of birth control."

"But they do make good rain gear for snakes," Chad piped in at that moment. He snickered.

"Chad Boily. What the heck are you doing?" I asked. "I don't remember anyone giving you permission to listen in on this."

Brian looked up at Chad and couldn't repress a chuckle. "They make great wind socks for midget weather stations, too," he quipped.

"'Cept for the weird lookin' ones with the secret compartment at the end," Chad said.

Caught off-guard, I shouted at him: "The what? Where do you pick this stuff up, mister?"

"Please don't encourage him," I said, under my breath, to Brian.

"Aw, Mom, I know about this stuff," Chad said.

"And I thought they'd be sheltered at a parochial

school," I whispered helplessly.

"It's everywhere," Brian pointed out.

When Chad asked Brian if he could keep several of the condoms, I objected. But Brian agreed, on the condition that they didn't leave the house. He pointed out that Chad was naturally curious, and he didn't want to be the one who squelched that healthy curiosity. He also felt that denying Chad's request would send the message that it was okay to be secretive about sex. I wasn't sure I agreed with him, but I gave in anyway.

The next day, Chad took one of the condoms to school with him.

"Guess what . . . I have a condom," he said to Jonathan, a boy a year younger than himself.

Jonathan smirked. "No way, you do not."

"Yes I do," Chad said, milking the hotshot's role for all he could squeeze from it.

"If you're serious, I'll buy it off you," Jonathan said.

"Okay, how much?" Chad asked.

"Give you five bucks for it."

Chad stealthily withdrew the condom from the pocket of his jeans. "You'll give me five bucks for this thing . . . sure . . . I'll sell it for five bucks."

"I can bring the money to school tomorrow," Jonathan promised.

"Yeah, okay," Chad said.

The next day, Jonathan told Chad that he'd find him at recess to seal the deal. But when the two of them met at the center of the schoolyard, Chad found out that fame wasn't always a good thing. A circle of onlookers quickly formed around them, because Jonathan had spread the word about Chad's possession.

It became an object lesson in the dangers of playing the bigshot. For the crowd of boys attracted an inquisitive girl into the circle, and her offended reaction was to bring the information about what she had witnessed to her teacher.

"Chad Boily, report to the office, immediately," came the announcement over the loudspeakers just minutes after recess ended.

With his track record of frequent illness, Chad hoped that it was only the school nurse checking up on his health. Since he was rarely, if ever, in trouble, he figured he had a shot at sliding by. But the stern face of the nun who greeted him just inside the office door quickly put an end to those hopes.

"Sit down, Chad," Sister Aurelia said. "I want you to tell me if you were trying to sell a toy to Jonathan."

For a minute, the nun's inability to be direct gave Chad the out he needed.

"No, Sister," he said. "I wasn't selling any toys."

"Well then, was there . . . anything . . . you were trying to sell him?"

"No, Sister," Chad said, "I really wasn't *trying* to sell anything." It was hard to argue with his logic. Since it was Jonathan who had suggested the sale, there had been no real salesmanship on Chad's part.

Frustrated, Sister Aurelia summoned Jonathan. "Were you two boys trying to make a deal?" she asked.

"Yes," Jonathan said.

"Yes, we were," Chad echoed, realizing he could no longer deny responsibility.

The nun nodded in satisfaction. "Okay, now I'd like to see the item for sale."

Chad pulled the condom from his pocket.

"Do you know what this is, Chad Boily?"

Chad nodded.

Handling it as though it were radioactive, Sister Aurelia deposited the condom in an envelope. "I'm going to have to phone your mother, Chad."

"Oh no, please Sister, anything but that," Chad pleaded.

I remember being summoned from my classroom and having to leave work early because my presence was absolutely required at *The Holy Cross School*.

I found Chad in the library, looking like a bank robber waiting to be called into a police lineup.

"I don't really understand this, Mrs. Boily," the principal, a short, round nun said. "Chad is usually one of the best-behaved children in school."

Feeling guilty, I explained the circumstances, emphasizing that we had forbidden Chad to remove the condoms from the house. The principal agreed that Chad would only be punished with a few days of detention, provided he presented her with a letter of apology. Although I went along, I felt obliged to add my own punishment for Chad's abuse of family trust. I grounded him for three months.

The condom-dealer incident was an exception, during which Chad strayed from his usually constructive approach to bringing interest into his life. For example, over the next several years, Chad became friends with a little boy, almost four years his junior, named Corey Worthington. He was the only other boy that lived on our block, and one day, on his walk home from the school-bus stop, Chad decided to introduce himself to the lonely looking five-year-old with the plastic sword.

Corey began to routinely appear at our apartment door. "Can Chad come play?" he would say, big blue eyes wide, button nose running.

"Chad's busy right now, Corey; I'll have to ask him, okay?" I said, grabbing a tissue to wipe his nose.

He smiled innocently. "Okay."

I knew that Chad was involved in one of his solo

projects and wasn't sure that he wanted to be bothered with someone so much younger than himself. I called into his room: "Chad, little Corey from up the block is here looking for you."

Chad appeared behind me in the kitchen. "It's okay, Mom; he can come in," he said.

Taking Corey by the hand, Chad led him toward his bedroom. "Come on, Corey . . . got some neat stuff to show you."

"Gee thanks, Chad. Sure glad I came over," Corey said.

What Chad had learned about "big-brothering" from his Uncles Dave and Jim, he used to improve the quality of Corey's childhood. Left out of activities by the kids at school, Chad would instead gladly play hide-and-seek and share his fascinating animal collection with his adopted little brother. Chad proved how much more mature he was than his so-called friends at school. He got tremendous satisfaction from caring for living things—whether it was little Corey, his baby cousins or his menagerie of small animals. It made me proud to be his mom; even when his love for living things became disruptive to the household.

Like the time I finally gave in to Chad's request to be allowed to add a snake to his collection of frogs, fish and lizards.

As he came inside from playing in the back yard one day, Chad held up a foot-long garter snake.

I knew it was harmless, but the hairs on the back of my neck bristled anyway; like many people, I just wasn't very comfortable with snakes.

"And where do you think you're going with that, Chad Boily?" I asked.

"Aw Mom, it's just a little one. Please . . . can I keep it . . . please?"

Against my better judgment, I agreed. "I'll give you one chance, Chad . . . only one. But if it ever gets out in the house, you're in deep trouble. I swear . . . I'll disown you."

"Don't worry, Mom, I'll take good care of it."

Off we went to the pet store, where we bought an inexpensive plastic box to serve as the snake observatory. The clerk warned us that the snake would also need a source of warmth, or else it wouldn't move or eat when winter came. But forking up twenty dollars for a warming stone was out of the question, budget-wise.

The snake and I coexisted without problems for about a month. But when Chad started to ask about the warming stone, I told him the snake would have to go.

"Oh please, Mom, I wanna take care of it. We've only had it a few weeks; can't we keep it?" he pleaded.

"Okay, Chad, but we'll have to figure out another way to warm it," I said.

We agreed on a solution. We'd move a small lamp into Chad's room and set the snake's case atop its shade.

Unfortunately, neither of us realized that the plastic would melt so easily. "Mom, Mom, my snake's gone," Chad said as he ran into the kitchen the next morning, his finger stuck through a hole in the plastic box.

"Oh my God," Amy said. "If he doesn't find that thing, I'm not sleeping in this house tonight, Mom."

"Everybody calm down," I said. "I'll find it before you come home from school." I felt the goose bumps rise on my arms.

I phoned the pet shop and was instructed to search anywhere that a source of heat was available—behind the refrigerator, in closets, near radiators. Concerned that it could enter a hole in the wall and make its way downstairs into my tenants' apartment, I decided not to tell them about it.

The following morning was trash day, and as I carried

the trash bags down the stairs, I was startled by a hissing sound above my head. Sliding from a hole in the stairwell ceiling, the darn snake fell to the stairs just below my foot. Unhurt, it slithered down the few remaining steps toward the space below my tenants' apartment door. I wanted to run the other way, but I knew I had to grab it. I stepped lightly on its rear end, picked it up, and headed for the back yard. When it coiled around my arm, I felt sure I was about to lose my breakfast.

As I opened the outer door and flung it outside, I heard a burst of laughter behind me. I looked back to see Chad at the top of the stairs. The part of me that felt foolish gave way to the sound of my son's laughter. Truth be told, I was at least as fond as my younger brothers of making Chad laugh.

♥ ♥ ♥

Unfortunately, neither uncles, nieces, adopted little brothers nor pets could blunt the edge of Chad's pain in his relationship with his father. There were just too many disappointments, too many failures to follow through. My husband would promise his children that he'd be home in time to take them somewhere—to a movie, to play miniature golf, or simply for an ice cream—and for whatever reason, would often show up an hour or two late.

"Sorry, I ran into a guy after work I haven't seen in a while, and I lost track of time," Amos would explain.

Years of frustration had lowered my daughter's tolerance for her father's excuses, and as she matured into an intelligent, responsible teenager, she began to tell him so. "No . . . no . . . I don't want to hear that, Dad," Amy hollered. "You always do this . . . always."

While my daughter raged, Chad would often disappear

into his room, where I or one of my brothers would find him in tears.

Sometimes, Amos would tell us that he was leaving for ten minutes to go up the street to a local store, then return several hours later. Each of these incidents had the same effect on Chad. At first, I assumed that he was crying over a broken promise, but later I came to realize that Chad's reaction was far more complicated. Chad wanted to spend time with his father; because he loved him; but also because he felt that his father needed his support.

"Memé, I have to be strong for him; he's only got me," Chad once confided to my mother, explaining how he was determined to help his father quit smoking and drinking.

Although he loved his son, it would be several more years before Amos realized just how much, and by that time it was too late for our marriage. One of the last straws was his push to enroll Chad in little league baseball. At first, I went along with the idea, because of my interest in seeing Chad better socialized with boys his own age. Baseball was a non-contact sport where Chad's heart would have an opportunity to recover from exertion as he stood in the field or sat in the dugout.

"You don't have to run a lot playing infield," Amos assured me.

"When are the games?" I asked.

"Saturday."

Saturday was nearly always either cake-baking day or cake-delivery day—or both. I knew we couldn't afford to be without the extra income that my little business produced—particularly during the summer when I was without my new teaching job. "Okay, we'll try it out . . . but only if you promise to get him to his games," I said.

"No problem," Amos said.

It wasn't long before shaking himself out of bed early

on Saturday became a problem for my husband, and Chad's stint as a little leaguer was over.

The whole idea of divorce cut against my basic beliefs. I was a staunch Catholic with a deep faith in God's love; I had been raised to regard marriage as a lifetime commitment. But after a year's separation, I felt I had to move on for both my own sake and for my children's.

♥ ♥ ♥

There wasn't a whole lot of monthly income standing between our family and poverty, and Chad's energy was going downhill again. Under the circumstances, meeting a significant other so soon after the breakup of my marriage was the furthest thing from my mind.

A combination of guilt, protectiveness toward my children and caution about my own vulnerability caused me to resist. But Brian was so consistent, so non-disruptive to our lives that he was impossible to dismiss as just another male on-the-make. His laid-back attitude allowed me the personal space I needed, and my discomfort evaporated in the glow of his genuinely warm smile. We began casually dating—dinner and a movie—and only on weekends. I could tell that my children were confused, but since our lives didn't change much, they seemed to accept it without major emotional upset.

Brian owned a condo on Old Orchard Beach, and it became a place of refuge for us that summer. Chad loved the seashore with its interesting marine life washed up on the sparkling white sand, and he seemed to find great peace in watching the cold Maine surf crash over the rocky coastline. We often took strolls along the beach, Chad pausing every so often to examine a sea urchin, or to collect a sand dollar. I felt more content than I had in many years.

It was during one of those walks that the reality of my son's condition jolted me like the waves tearing at that beach during a Nor'easter. After just a few minutes at a leisurely pace, Chad knelt down on the sand as he often did when there was a seaweed, animal or tidal pool to study.

I checked out the area around him but couldn't see anything interesting. "What did you find, Chad?" I asked.

"Mom, I don't feel good," he said.

I knelt next to him in the sand. It was hard to see in the evening shadows, but his lips looked darker than usual, and his breathing seemed more labored. I put my arms around him. "What's the matter honey?"

"Mom . . . I can't breathe," he said, squinting in pain.

"Oh no, my poor honey," I said. "Can you walk back to Brian's okay?"

He shook his head. "Don't know, Mom."

"How 'bout a ride, boss," Brian said. Stretching out his arms, he lifted Chad's small body onto his shoulders.

I had no way of knowing it then, but that walk was symbolic of the many times Brian would be there for us in the months and years to come.

Although Chad slowly regained his breath that day, there would be many more times over that winter when he would struggle for oxygen, many days he would miss school because he could hardly get out of bed without becoming exhausted. His amazing, but terribly damaged heart could no longer keep up with the rest of his body.

"Some things haven't changed, Mrs. Boily. Red and blue blood still mix freely inside Chad's heart," Doctor McFaul told me after a catheterization performed at M.M.C. in early 1989.

"Then why—"

"Probably because he's getting bigger while his heart's really not," the doctor said. "Possibly because the valve shared by the right and left sides has become mildly insufficient."

"Insufficient?"

"It's leaking a little, making Chad's heart an even less efficient pump than it already was."

As I swallowed, I felt like a wad of paper was stuck in my throat. Valve problems meant surgery—even I knew that. And we'd been able to avoid surgery since that unbearable two weeks in Chad's third month of life. I was terrified.

"Is he going to need valve surgery?" I asked.

Doctor McFaul shook his head. "Valves can't be strengthened, only replaced. And with the abnormal position of the valve, and the situation in the remainder of Chad's heart, valve replacement really isn't an option."

For an instant, I relaxed. No surgery—maybe there were new and stronger drugs that could help Chad.

Doctor McFaul adjusted the position of his eyeglasses. "We've reached the point where the only viable option is the single-ventricle repair surgery—you know, the Fontan procedure . . . the one we've spoken about in the past. It involves a reconstruction of the way Chad's heart works."

"Oh God," I said. "I thought you said it carried a high risk."

"It does, but the success rate is far better now than it was five years ago. For example, they've done about a dozen in Boston with only one complication that I'm aware of."

"Boston?"

"We're not equipped to do it here. I've already set up a cardiology visit for you at Children's. Naturally their opinion about this course of action may differ from mine."

I dug my fingernails into the skin of my forearm, terrified to pose a question I knew I had to ask. "How much time could this give Chad, Doctor McFaul? I mean, could he live 'til thirty, for instance?"

He managed a small smile. "You know, Mrs. Boily, he could outlive you and me . . . he could live to be sixty." He massaged his forehead. "Then again, he might not. We just don't know."

"But what about children who've had the operation?"

"Some have done very well." He shrugged. "But it's such a new procedure . . ."

The rest was left unsaid. There just wasn't much information on survival after the Fontan surgery. But I had to have something positive to hang my courage on, so I focused on the first part of Doctor McFaul's answer—that Chad might even outlive me. It made me realize how little faith I had ever had in that possibility.

Thankfully, Doctor McFaul didn't tell me everything. In a letter to Chad's pediatrician, he warned: "My biggest concern relates to the degree of valve insufficiency. If this valve leak is moderate . . . the Fontan operation would be hazardous."

In spite of my own uncertainty, I was put in the position of trying to convince Amos that Chad needed the operation. Amos loved Chad dearly, but he also dwelled on the possibility of losing him. During late winter of 1989, just about everyone we knew offered an opinion about what each sincerely believed was the best course of action.

As always, it ended up being my decision. After almost nine years, it was time to go to Boston again.

CHAPTER SIX:
The Second Heart

I had just turned nine, and there was plenty of bogus news in my life. My parents' divorce was definitely kicking my butt. But the major horror show was the way I felt every morning.

While other kids were cruising off to school, I was getting zonked with heart failure. Nobody was saying it that way—at least not around me. But looking back, I know that's what was going down. I had almost no energy and felt like I was always struggling to breathe. And getting my brain in gear for school got harder and harder. I was *weesh*—all I wanted to do was chill. Air-guitar playing was definitely out of the question.

That spring, on a perfect day for waking up lawns and daffodils, Mom and I drove down to Boston. We took the elevator up to the sixth floor of Children's Hospital, where we met Doctor Keane, my Boston cardiologist. White hair, red face and an epic smile—he reminded me of Saint Nick minus the beard. Instead of the red suit, he wore a long white coat.

"You must be Chad," Doctor Keane said softly, as he patted my head. He brought us to a cool room with some striped sofas and blue chairs and introduced us to Doctor Richard Jonas. Dark-haired and thin, he looked too young to be a cardiac surgeon. Compared to Doctor Keane, Doctor J. was high-voltage; super-charged.

"Doctor Jonas has performed several successful Fontan surgeries," Doctor Keane said.

As she shook the surgeon's hand, my mom hesitated. I guess she was trying to feel something about his connection with God.

I was blown away by how cool Doctor Jonas was about the operation. I've always had a lot of respect for doctors, especially the ones who know how to talk to patients. Even at nine, I could already peg Doctor J. for a major dude.

Doctor J. and Doctor K. did a tag-team rap, trying to explain the Fontan procedure to Mom and me. Since red and blue blood mixed inside my heart, something had to be done to separate them, so the blood going out to my brain, muscles and other organs would be redder—so it would have more oxygen. Doctor J. would stick a piece of Teflon in the upper right chamber of my heart, just like a separator between the tweeter and woofer in a speaker box. The Teflon would force the blue blood from my body directly to my lungs. This would stop any of that blue blood from passing into the lower part of my heart, where because of the hole there, it usually mixed with the red blood coming back from my lungs.

After the surgery, there would be only red blood in my ventricles, and both those lower pumps—left and right— could work together, pumping that red blood into my arteries. The strong right side would be able to help the left side do the job it was too *weesh* to do alone. In some ways, this turned my four-chambered heart into a three-chambered pump, sort of like the heart of frogs. I have sometimes wondered if my love of frogs when I was a little kid might not have been a message from God about what was coming in my life.

I wasn't really scared of the operation, because I was willing to try whatever the doctors thought would jump-start my energy. My biggest worry after that meeting with Doctors

Keane and Jonas was that I was about to lose a big chunk of my summer vacation in the hospital.

Unfortunately, everybody else was blown away by the Fontan. I could see it in Mom's eyes, knew it from the way my grandmother started telling everybody to pray, even before I went into the hospital.

Most of all, I could hear it in my sister's voice: "Oh my God, Mom, they're going to do open-heart surgery," Amy said.

The Fontan surgery was the first time my sister really realized how sick I was. Mom had always protected her, so her life wouldn't be twisted by my illness. But Amy was a brain, an ace student, and now she had studied enough biology to make the connections on her own.

My mother spazzed. "Yes, Amy I guess that's right," she mumbled.

Of course, they would have to open my heart to insert the divider, but no one had put it in those words before. Since my infant surgery had been limited to outside-the-heart repairs, open-heart surgery raised the stakes. And with her new interest in science, my sister had dealt the hand face-up.

"No wonder he's going to be on the machine," Amy said, the dimples in her face showing through her stranged-out expression.

"Machine?" Mom said.

Amy spread her arms to indicate something huge. "The heart-lung machine, Mom."

"Is that what Doctor Jonas was talking about?"

"Yeah, but he called it a 'Cardio-something-something machine," I said. "Amy looked it up."

"Cardio-Pulmonary Bypass," Amy said.

The corners of Mom's mouth sagged. "What does it do?"

I could tell that my mother didn't really want to ask the question. But she felt like she had to be on top of every detail, like anything less would be a cop-out.

My sister traced a loop in the air with her finger. "The machine takes Chad's blood and puts oxygen into it . . . like his lungs would normally do . . . then pumps it back into his body."

"Unbelievable . . . so he's not breathing while he's on it?"

"No, Mom," Amy said, "it wouldn't do any good for him to breathe. There's no blood going to his lungs anyway."

My mother's eyes said it all. The thought of my life being dependent on the Bypass machine was hardcore. I wouldn't be breathing God's life-giving oxygen into my lungs. It was like my soul temporarily passed from God's hands into the hands of technology, a mind-boggling idea to her.

As we got closer to the operation, the stress got worse and worse. I could hardly sleep, thinking about the parts of the patient gig that I already knew well—the blood drawing, poking and prodding; the IVs, tubes and wires that make moving around impossible; the boring down-time; the bogus food. I asked my mother if she would keep me company until I fell asleep. And just as she had done when I was an infant, she slept in my room every night that last week before the surgery, encouraging me, promising me that I would feel much better.

I remember only one time before the operation when I really got bent out of shape. I was talking to my friend, Corey, just before my admission to the hospital. When I look back, it flips-me-out that a six-year-old kid was so tuned-in.

"You comin' home soon, Chad?" Corey asked.

"Doctors said maybe two, three weeks."

"But we gonna play some more, right?" His blue eyes looked as big as Frisbees.

"Sure, Corey . . . teach you some new magic tricks, or we can play swords . . . or go lookin' for snakes . . . or whatever."

"But 'pose you're in heaven, Chad? Can I come and play there?"

"I'm not really sure what people do in heaven, Corey, but I guess we all get to go there sooner or later," I said.

That conversation must have dug up something I had buried deep in my mind; because a few days later, I asked my mother my own version of Corey's question.

We were decorating the house for a party that was her way of cheering me up. Mom figured that making decoration stuff for the party would keep my mind occupied; then I'd get a chance to see almost everybody I knew before the operation.

"The decorations really look great, don't they, Chad?" Mom said as I helped her tape streamers over our kitchen table.

"Yup," I said.

My eyes drifted from the corner of the room toward the patio sliders that led to a small deck outside our kitchen. I stared out at the sky and thought about God. "Mom, does God really make special places for people in heaven?" I asked.

My mother dropped the roll of tape. She looked really bent out of shape. It seemed like forever before she answered. "Oh yes, Chad," she said. "God makes all sorts of special places for people."

She climbed down from her chair and grabbed my shoulders, holding me at arm's length. "Honey, why are you asking?"

"I just wonder if He's gonna make a special place for

me in heaven, Mom."

Mom hugged me as hard as she could. "Chad . . . He's going to make a special place for us *all* in heaven, and I'll make sure yours is *extra special*, 'cause I'll be there *before* you."

My mother's bravery in facing all the hard-core stuff in our lives was one of the major reasons I even got as far as the Fontan operation. Sure, there were the docs and the drugs and all the rest of the medical stuff, but without Mom's courage, I would have never hung-in-there that long.

The pre-Fontan party was a rush. There was a ton of food, and Mom had planned enough indoor and outdoor activities to keep everybody hopping. It didn't make me any less of a *zeke* among the kids I knew, but it did take everybody's mind off the operation.

♥ ♥ ♥

Brian became a major dude during my Fontan surgery. I could tell how much he loved Mom and how he helped keep her together at bad times. No way he'd ever replace Dad, but he didn't try either. He was always laid-back with Amy and me. It was like he was saying: "This is who I am, I hope we can be friends."

Brian took charge when they were admitting me to Children's and the nurse asked whether we wanted a tour of the I.C.U.

"It's an option we offer parents so they'll be better prepared . . . know what to expect," the nurse said to my mother.

Mom turned to Brian. "Do we really want to do this?" she asked.

"What do you think, boss?" Brian asked.

"I think I wanna go," I said.

"Are you sure, honey?" Mom said. "You might see things you might not really want to see in there . . . maybe some scary things. But remember . . . all these kids are being taken care of and they'll be much better after their operations."

"Mom, I know I'm gonna be much better after mine, too," I said. It wasn't like I was clueless. I really believed what I was saying.

"I think we should go," Brian said.

I know that my mother thought I was being brave. But I wasn't nearly as scared of the surgery as I was about what other people were feeling—all the other people who had been helping me pull through; who never copped-out on me, never let me down. I loved my mom so much, and I knew that seeing all those kids hooked up to I.V.s, machines, and breathing tubes wasn't going to be easy for her. I had to be there to hold her hand like she'd always been there to hold mine.

Luckily, no one Coded during the tour, and clutching Brian's hand on one side and mine on the other, my mother made it through with her hand still steady enough to sign the papers for the operation.

"You're going to be better after this, honey," she said with a smile.

"I know, Mom," I said. At that moment, we both really believed we had found an answer.

CHAPTER SEVEN:
Alex

It was during the pre-op for my Fontan surgery when I first figured it out: Sure I was a patient, but I was also a major practice dummy. Just about every kind of trainee—from Mickey Mouse-eared Child Life specialists to cardiology residents—got their shot at trying out their stuff on me. I guess my heart was such a freak-show, a one-of-a-kinder, that they all needed a crack at me.

Usually, it didn't bother me much, but this time, the nurse-anesthetist trainee was so out-there, that I got sick-to-my-stomach from the pain of her bogus needle-sticks. *I'm supposed to pass out from the drug you're giving me, not from the pain of being injected with it*, I thought. Heck, I already had extra holes *inside* my body.

Knowing that my mother would need lots of spiritual support, a major chunk of our family came together in the surgical waiting area on the day of the operation. Everybody who could skip-out, shave or trade-off work hours showed up in that waiting room to count down the hours with Mom. From my Uncle Vinny who taught biology at a college up the street to my grandfather who had to use-up a fire-department vacation day to be there, the family came through as usual—to help Mom deal with the kid-on-the-machine.

At 3:15 p.m., after about five hours of surgery, Doctor Jonas flew into the waiting room, a partly open green surgical gown trailing him like Superman's cape.

"He came through the surgery fine," Doctor J. said to Mom. "He's currently being supported by the heart-lung machine."

"Then he's gonna be all right," my father said.

Doctor J. nodded. "We anticipate so."

"What do you mean, 'you *anticipate*'?" Mom asked.

"We won't know how the Fontan heart is performing until we take Chad off the machine and let it function without assistance," Doctor Jonas said.

The next few hours were major stressful for my family. It was like my soul would pass back into God's hands when they disconnected me from the machine, but no one knew whether I would be with God on earth or in heaven.

I don't think God ever really let go of me during that post-op. I awoke from a dream in which I was running down the length of a field, kicking a ball toward a goal, wind at my face, sun at my back, guardian angels floating on each side of me.

The dream filled me with hope that the surgery had gone well. Unfortunately, when I tried to breathe, I felt only pain in both sides of my chest. Twisting my head, I saw the three tubes sticking out of my body. No one had warned me about this part of it. I had no idea what to think.

"Chad, it's Mom," I heard my mother's voice nearby, and I felt the gentle touch of her hand.

I stuck out my tongue. It was the coolest way to let her know that I was basically okay. She caught-a-chuckle from it, which made me feel better.

"You little bugger," Mom said. "How do you feel?"

"Lookin' good, bum," my father encouraged.

Mom pointed toward the glass wall that separated my room from the main area of the Cardiac Intensive Care Unit. "Everyone's here, Chad."

Turning my head, I saw a group of familiar faces. They

were smiling and waving—sending their prayers in my direction.

"Mom, it hurts to breathe," I said. I pointed at the chest tubes.

"I know, honey; Doctor Jonas is on his way to tell you about that."

"There's some fluid around your lungs that's a result of the surgery, Chad," a nurse chimed-in from behind my mother. "The fluid doesn't just make it harder to breathe, but it also puts an extra strain on your heart. While your heart heals, we'll need to drain it every so often."

"That's what the tubes are for, honey," Mom said. "Don't worry, they're only temporary."

Those chest tubes were probably the most bogus medical treatment I ever remember getting. It's not that I didn't need them; it's just that they were so incredibly painful. Every time the resident showed in my room with that giant suctioning syringe, I'd go completely *postal*, trying to convince him not to use it on me. I would cough for fifteen minutes after the doc finished suctioning. It felt like I was puking my lungs out, and once or twice, I did vomit from my stomach after my lungs got through puking. I was ugly for at least a day after every suctioning—didn't want to talk to *anybody*.

♥ ♥ ♥

I had met Alex the night before my Fontan surgery. A six-year-old princess with blue eyes and golden hair, she was a major cutie, a sweetheart. But I could tell that we belonged to the same club. She was small for her age and her skin color was more purple than pink. Her parents looked flipped-out about her; I'd seen the same look on my mom's face a hundred times.

"Hi, my name's Alex," she said, with an epic smile.

She was a little young to be my first love, but I knew I wanted to see that smile again, and that I had the voltage to jump-start it. "I'm Chad," I said. "I'm having Fontan surgery tomorrow."

Alex's dad bent over to kiss the top of her head. "Alex is here for a Fontan, too," he said.

I thought about Alex every day, as I lay in bed after surgery with those chest tubes sucking my energy. One night, after I had been discharged from intensive care, her dad came by to visit me.

"Hi Chad, you're looking great. How do you feel?" he said.

"Okay, I guess. 'Cept for these stupid tubes. How's Alex?" I asked.

"Not so good, I'm afraid. Her surgery turned out to be more complicated than yours was. Doctor Jonas is pretty worried about her. He says it's touch-and-go, right now."

"Oh my God," my mom said. "You've got to believe she's going to pull through."

Alex's dad looked like he was struggling not to cry in front of us. "I'm trying to believe that, Mrs. Boily. And praying as hard as I know how," he said.

"We're praying too, right Chad?" Mom said.

Alex's dad put his hand on my shoulder. "Alex is asking for you, Chad. I know it would cheer her up if you could visit . . . as soon as you're feeling up to it. Meanwhile, you keep on fighting to get better." He squeezed my shoulder and left the room.

My brain locked-on to a cool idea. "Mom . . . wouldn't it be great if I could do magic for Alex . . . and the other kids too?"

Mom was psyched. "I could bring down some of your stuff this weekend," she said.

"But Mom, that's three days away. Alex needs to be cheered up, now," I said.

Sitting in a corner of the room, my sister threw in her two cents: "Why don't you try the gift shop. I saw all sorts of magic stuff in there, yesterday."

The gift shop was a great idea. They had all sorts of cool stuff—from trick decks of cards to disappearing coins. I psyched myself up. Putting together a traveling magic show was a lot better than lying around, bored.

Alex was my biggest fan, but I also had a big audience from the other kids and the nurses. For a while, I did a show just about every other day—sometimes in the game room, at other times in the room of a very sick kid. There was no doubt that every *ooh* and *aah* was a burst of positive energy that helped my own healing. And when the tricks bombed like they sometimes did, the giggles reminded me that success or failure was less important than getting smiles out of kids as sick or sicker than I was. Heck, I giggled more than they did. If they didn't mind me screwing-up, why should I?

But from Alex, there was even more. Alex temporarily adopted me as her big brother, and God allowed me to help her heal. Not only did I do magic, but I also showed her how the tricks were done. And by revealing my magician's "secrets," I somehow opened another door. We talked about our lives—what they had been and what we hoped they would be.

I was blown-away by how much we had in common. "Do you ever ask God to help you be normal . . . like the other kids?" she asked me.

"Sometimes," I said. "Wish I could play soccer and hockey with the other kids . . . . and with my uncles."

"Think you ever will?"

"Hope so. It's kinda why I was up for the Fontan. What about you?"

"I know God loves me," she said. "But I don't know if I'll ever be like other kids."

"Guess you're always different when your heart is sick," I said. "But I don't think God loves us any less."

Her eyes glistened. "My dad says he thinks God must love me more . . . because so many people pray for me every day."

"Um . . . I guess that must be true. I know how many people pray for me . . . and it's a lot."

"I pray for you, Chad," she said.

My Fontan heart wiggled inside my chest. I wanted to hug her, but I was still too much of a dork. "Thanks, I pray for you too," I said.

Whether it was prayers, magic or just God's love, Alex managed to out-heal me. The cardiologists decided that she was ready to leave while I was still a week away from getting rid of my chest tubes. When I heard that I was staying, I got as twisted as I can ever remember. I did a major cop-out; threw all my magic stuff into a corner and refused to perform.

"Aren't you going to entertain the kids today, Chad?" my mother asked.

"No, Mom, I don't feel like it. Don't think I'll ever feel like it again."

For three days, I refused to budge. On the fourth day, Alex came into my room. It was the day before her discharge, and she wanted one last magic show.

"I'm not doing magic today, Alex," I said.

"Not even for me, Chad . . . for my last time before I leave?"

"Sorry, I can't."

"Sure you can, Chad. Come on . . . *please*."

"Okay," I said. "I do have a new trick I could show everybody." Nobody except Alex could have unbent me enough to convince me to perform.

Her parents let me know that they really believed I had helped Alex get better. They brought her to my room just before they left the hospital.

"I gotta go now, Chad," Alex said from her wheelchair. "I wish I could stay until you got out, too."

"It's okay. I'm outta here soon," I said.

"Thanks so much for being Alex's friend, Chad," her father said.

I got all choked-up, and my mom had to answer for me. "I know Chad really enjoyed spending time with Alex," she said.

"Uh huh," I said, nodding.

"Don't forget what you wanted to give Chad," Alex's father said to her.

Alex held out her hand. "I want you to have this to remember me by, Chad." She handed me a wallet-size picture.

As usual, Mom came through for me, digging through her purse until she found a recent photo of me. "I'm sure Chad would like you to have this, Alex."

"I'll never forget you, Chad," Alex said, blue eyes dancing. "Will you remember me?"

"Sure thing," I said. I wanted to tell her what a great kid she was, how much her good energy had meant to me; that I had done the magic more for her than for anybody else. But I just waved good-bye as her dad backed her wheelchair out of my room.

The fluid draining from my chest never really stopped, but I was finally cleared for discharge near the end of August. Doctor Keane told us that the fluid might still have to be drained on an outpatient basis. At least it was "outpatient." I'd been in the hospital for a month, and anything was better than staying there even one more day.

That final day in the hospital, I had one last tangle with

the tubes of pain. I was visited by two *dirtbags* I'd never seen before—docs or nurses, I'm not even sure. Whoever they were, they were on the goon squad. Standing on either side of my bed, they latched-on to the tubes and yanked them from my chest. I yelled like feedback from a two-hundred-watt amp turned up to ten.

One of my nurses ran into my room. She began stroking my head. "I can only *imagine* how much it must hurt, Chad," she said. "But believe me, you're not yelling half as loud as some other patients I've had . . . children *and* adults."

I gritted my teeth and tried to chill. "Why the heck didn't they tell me what they were gonna do?" I asked.

"Because they think it's easier on you if they just get it over with. It's sort of standard procedure."

"Well, they're wrong," I said. "I like to know what's happening to me, so I can get ready for it."

"I'm sorry they hurt you so much, Chad," the nurse said, squeezing my hand.

"It's not your fault," I said. At least the tubes were finally out of my body.

♥ ♥ ♥

It was a totally muggy Sunday in September. Thankful for the air conditioning in Brian's Jeep, I chilled-out for the ride up to Lewiston. All my discharge meds were different diuretics to control fluid buildup, so I would be living without the heart-muscle strengthener, Lanoxin, for just about the first time. My skin color was pretty decent overall. My Fontan heart seemed to be doing its job.

The Fontan heart's only strangeness was the way it sounded. Instead of a "thump," my heart's sound was mushier, more like a *gwoosh*. Doctor Keane said it was like a car engine with sticky valves—blood flow through my heart wasn't as smooth as it was in a completely normal one.

On the drive back to Maine, I couldn't help feeling bummed about the loss of my summer. School was about to start, and I wasn't at all ready to go back. Plus, I'd be missing at least the first week, maybe more, so I'd be behind the other kids again.

Almost everybody in my family came to visit during those first few days at home. On Wednesday, my Uncle Jimmy took time out of his busy school, sports and work schedule to come over for the evening. Every year seemed to bring new challenges into Jim's life, and since he was less and less available, I was really psyched to see him. I knew we'd probably shoot pool or play some video games, but somewhere deep inside me, I held onto the hope that soon, with my souped-up heart, I might be playing soccer or hockey with him.

"Hey buddy, how 'bout I kick your butt at Eight Ball after dinner?" Jim said from his chair near the kitchen door.

"Just don't overdo it," Mom said to Jim from across the dinner table. "Chad's supposed to be resting until he goes back to school."

"Aw Mom, it's just pool," I said. I buried my fork in a mound of mashed potatoes, psyched to taste the real thing after a month of bogus hospital plastic-food.

I never got to taste that awesome mouthful. I had barely raised my fork to chest level when I lost control of my arm. The fork fell back to my plate, splattering food toward my sister across the table.

Amy was ticked. "That's not funny, Chad," she said.

My mother saw the panic in my face. "Chad, what's wrong . . . what's happening, honey?" She stared at my arm lying on the table.

Gritting my teeth, I commanded my arm to move, but it was Jello. I started to flip-out; even a bad heart was better than being paralyzed.

"Mom, I can't move my arm," I said. I tried to stand, but my right leg buckled under me. Throwing out my left arm, I latched onto my Uncle Jim. He reached out and grabbed me before I fell backward into the glass patio slider.

Mom dialed Doctor Keane's number in Boston. A cardiologist on-duty told her to take me to Portland. About an hour later, I was admitted to Maine Medical Center— just three days after my discharge from Children's Hospital.

CHAPTER EIGHT:
Oh Lord, Not My
Brain!

My right arm and leg felt like they had been trapped under my body all night. Tingling with "pins and needles," they seemed like fake rubber limbs that didn't really belong to me. I had no idea what was happening, but naturally, I figured that my brand new Fontan heart had already crapped-out, taken a long lunch break. I was down to three chambers. Maybe it wasn't going to cut it.

A tall man with a thick brown mustache came into my cubicle in the M.M.C. Emergency Room and said he was Doctor Sargent, the neurology resident. He started poking, swiping and beating-on me with a little silver hammer. *Bang-bang*, it was truly strange.

The neurologists kept at it for two days, but they were still clueless. So Doctor McFaul ordered an echocardiogram.

"Do you think Chad's new heart is having problems already?" my mom asked.

Doctor McFaul shook his head. "No, the heart seems to be functioning well, Mrs. Boily. I'm simply being cautious . . . trying to cover all bases."

He couldn't be sure, but Doctor McFaul thought he saw blood clots inside my new Fontan heart—right where Doctor J. had put the Teflon divider. So he added Coumadin, a strong blood thinner to my list of meds. Then he sent us back to Boston.

We found out later that I had had what's called a T.I.A.—a brief block in blood flow to a piece of my brain. Since there were probably clots forming in my heart, it's possible that one of them, maybe a small one, broke away and traveled in the bloodstream until it reached my brain and temporarily blocked an artery.

After another week of poking, blood-drawing and echocardiograms, the docs at Children's decided they agreed with Doctor McFaul's diagnosis about the clots in my heart. They discharged me on a protective blood-thinning combo of Coumadin and aspirin. I guess they wanted my blood to flow like five-weight oil.

I was already three weeks behind in school. And my new heart was kind of useless, because now I had to worry about bleeding like a garden snake in a lawn mower. I started finding bruises all over my body. But what flipped me out was brushing my teeth. The red foam poured out of my mouth every time I ran a toothbrush across my gums. So we knew that if I cut myself playing outside, the bleeding might never stop.

Then the nosebleeds started. Each began as an itch in one of my nostrils, followed by the sensation that my nose was beginning to run. It was almost like I was having an allergic reaction. I rubbed a tissue across my nose, expecting to wipe some clear fluid. But the tissue was bright red. I felt like Bruce Lee's practice dummy.

"Mom, my nose is bleeding," I hollered, on my way to the bathroom.

By the time my mother got there, the blood was flooding from my nose directly into the sink drain. "Oh Lord, Chad, what did you do?" Mom asked.

"Nothing, Mom, it just started by itself. Check it out." I pointed to a wad of bloody tissues in the waste paper basket.

She handed me a towel. "Hold this against your nose

and put on as much pressure as you can."

Mom plastered some cotton with Vaseline, made me lie down with my head back and did her best to plug my nose.

"Okay, honey, bring the towel; we're going to the emergency room," she said.

It kept happening—over and over again—that winter. I'm sure the docs and nurses at C.M.M.C. must have gotten tired of seeing me with a bloody towel against my face.

For some reason, about that same time, I got pumped-up by those mushy ketchup containers that they give you at fast-food joints. I was into trying to figure out why they acted the way they did. It was like hands-on physics at Burger King.

I guess it was my science-*dweeb* phase. I got some sort of weird rush from twisting those little suckers to squeeze the insides, then stomping on them to squirt a stream of ketchup under pressure.

Of course, I usually got my strange thrills outside the house, but one time—when I couldn't sleep—I decided to fool around with the ketchup packs in bed. Bored with my old bedroom, I had convinced Mom to let me move upstairs to the third floor dormer where Uncle Jim used to get my head-banging wake-up calls.

Unfortunately, that night, I turned one twist too many. A pinhole opened in the package, squirting tiny bursts of ketchup, like small-caliber machine-gun fire, onto the slanted ceiling of the dormer. The ceiling was white and textured, so I had no luck trying to mop up the evidence. There were plenty of stains left behind in the plaster. I figured I'd tell Mom that the roof had leaked, but I doubted she'd buy such a lame story.

The next morning, I was awakened by the sound of my

mother's frantic voice. "Chad, what happened? Did you bleed again last night? This is unbelievable." She pointed at the ceiling.

For a minute, I couldn't figure out what she was getting at, but as my brain jump-started, I remembered the ketchup stains.

"Gee, Mom, I wasn't bleeding; I can't tell you how those got there," I said like a dork.

"Then where did they come from? Certainly not the angels?"

"Yeah, Mom; must've been the angels," I said with a grin. "They're the only ones could've come through the ceiling without cracking the plaster, right?"

Mom didn't catch any chuckles from my lame joke. "Come on, Chad," she said. "I know boys of your age like to experiment . . . did you do something that didn't turn out the way you thought?"

I decided to fess-up. "It's not the angels, Mom. It's ketchup," I said. I spent the first two hours after school scrubbing those stains, and I never did any physics experiments in the house again—not with ketchup, anyway.

It was too bad I couldn't rent an angel to stop my nosebleeds. Doctor McFaul was bent out of shape about them, because he thought I might be bleeding inside. So he did another echocardiogram to check on the clotting problem in my heart. When the test came up zeros, he called Children's to get their angle on my case.

"Mrs. Boily, according to Doctor Jonas, no late cerebrovascular events have been observed in any of his other Fontan patients," Doctor McFaul said to Mom, after that phone call to Boston.

"I don't understand what that means, Doctor McFaul," Mom said.

"It means that once children like Chad have fully

recovered from the surgery, there's been no further clot formation observed," Doctor McFaul said. "Since his heart is currently clear of clots, Doctor Jonas seems confident that we're past any danger point."

"So he can come off the Coumadin?"

"Yes . . . and the daily aspirin as well. We'll be discontinuing all anticoagulant therapy. This should stop the nosebleeds."

"All right," I shouted. I was psyched. Maybe I could finally do some of the things I'd never had the energy for. Doctor McFaul told me that my heart's valve was leaking, but he didn't make it sound like anything major.

"Mom, I'd like to learn karate," I said on the ride home from Portland.

"I don't know, Chad. Let me think about it and ask around to see who's holding classes. Besides, you need to catch up in school first."

I worked hard to make up missed schoolwork that fall of 1989, and I felt better than ever. I was still smaller than other kids my age and still got zonked easily, but I was psyched for the first time in a long time. I had a couple of friends who seemed to like me for who I was, and they made up for the others who still treated me like I was some kind of interplanetary *zeke*.

♥ ♥ ♥

It was Thanksgiving week, and I had a lot to be thankful for. I woke up remembering that my dad and cousins were taking me out for the day and evening, and I was really psyched to see them.

Jumping out of bed, I rushed downstairs to see if my father might already be waiting for me in the kitchen. When I saw that he wasn't, I headed upstairs to practice my pool stroke. I imagined I was playing Eight Ball with my Uncle Jim. *Bang, bang, bang*, I pocketed three striped balls in a row; I was kicking butt.

Then, the strangest feeling hit me. Suddenly, my vision started to fuzz. There were two pool tables, then three. I popped-up the cue ball like a rookie, sending it into the corner of the room. Then I lost my balance, staying on my feet only by grabbing on to the table rail. Flipping-out, I got on my hands and knees and crawled to the stairs.

"Mom . . . Mom," I yelled.

I used the handrail to pull myself to my feet, but when the stairwell started flipping sideways, I flopped onto the floor again and started crawling down the stairs.

Then the world turned completely upside-down.

"Where's my mom. I want my mom," I yelled as loudly as I could.

"My God, Chad; what's the matter?" I heard Mom's voice say.

"I want my mom; I want my mom," I repeated. "Mom, Mom, please help me."

"Calm down, honey, I'm right here," my mother said as she helped me to my feet at the bottom of the stairs.

"No . . . no . . . I want my mother," I kept saying.

"I'm right here, Chad. It's okay." She hugged me tightly, brought me into her room and sat me down on the bed. "It's okay, honey, I'm here," she said.

"No, no, I want my mom," I continued to holler, like a total brick-brain. I couldn't recognize her; had no idea who this person was. It was a really bad scene.

It was like I had split into two personalities. One had contact with the past and remembered shooting pool. The other came into being from a space-time fracture in the stairwell and had no history in this continuum. It was the weirdest feeling I have ever known.

Mom later told me that my eyes were fixed in a Zombie-like stare, while I kept yelling at her that I wanted my mother. She was so flipped-out that she called Brian, because she didn't think she was going to be able to drive the ten minutes to the C.M.M.C. emergency room.

Mom was even more bent out of shape by the time we got to the hospital. I had quieted down, but my eyes were still in Voodoo-ville. I was zoned-out, big-time.

A resident started to poke at my body, and he swiped a wicked-cold metal wheel across the soles of my feet. "Chad, we're going to use a machine that's sort of like a very fancy X-ray to have a look inside your brain," he said. "Do you understand?"

I shrugged. "I guess so."

"How are you feeling right now?" the doctor asked.

"I'm not myself," I said.

"You mean you don't feel quite as well as you'd like?"

"*No*, I mean I don't feel like *me*. I feel like somebody else . . . somebody I don't know."

"He's been saying that ever since we got out of the car," my mother said.

Neither the C.T. scan nor the neurology exam showed anything wrong, but Doctor Marsh, my pediatrician, looked like he thought I was headed for a dirt-nap. He figured it had to be my brain, and he told Mom that sometimes blood flow problems in the brain didn't show up right away. They rushed me to M.M.C. by ambulance.

The next morning, I snapped out of my fog and was able to recognize Mom, Brian and Amy. But when I tried to reach over and grab a paper cup filled with water, I knocked it to the floor instead. And when I tried to talk, everything sounded like some bogus language that nobody had ever heard. My lips and tongue felt like they were all glued together.

I spent Thanksgiving and the first week of the Christmas season at M.M.C. The nurses were great, bringing me turkey and fixings. But I wasn't very hungry, especially when I found out how clumsy my right hand was with a fork. I wasn't having any trouble understanding words and knowing what words I wanted to say, but actually saying them was a major horror-show.

After another C.T. scan, the M.M.C. neurologists decided I'd had a blood-vessel blockage in the cerebellum, an area of my brain that played a big part in coordinating movements like writing and talking.

"Chad, I'm sorry to have to tell you this," Doctor McFaul said. "But it looks like you've suffered a minor stroke."

"This is unbelievable," my mother said. "How could this happen?"

"Possibly a clot that formed inside his heart then traveled to his brain," Doctor McFaul said.

"You mean from the Fontan?" Mom said, sounding more bent with every second.

"I thought the operation was supposed to make him better," my father said from behind her. Dad was really ripped.

"Why don't we all calm down and let Doctor McFaul explain," Brian said. He took Doctor McFaul and my parents into the hallway outside my room, and left my sister and my grandparents behind with me.

I wouldn't totally appreciate how cool Brian was until a few years later. He knew that the worst thing others could do was confuse me with negativity. He knew I needed to be told what was going down. But he also figured that everybody had to be laid-back about it, so I could deal with the bogus story line my life was following. It wasn't that Brian was unsympathetic or unemotional. He just realized that after ten years of learning to live with a bad heart, I had suddenly been zonked with something much scarier—brain damage.

When everybody came back into my room, Doctor McFaul gave his explanation. My stroke was minor, and with physical and occupational therapy, the docs felt I could recover both speech and writing. Because of the weird position and leakiness of my shared heart valve, there could be a danger of clots forming around it. So I would have to be put back onto blood thinners. Maybe forever.

Doctor McFaul put his hand on my shoulder. "I know I took you off the Coumadin, Chad . . . but that was to stop the nosebleeds and allow you to be more active . . . to enjoy your new heart. So when Doctor Jonas advised me that Fontan patients didn't really need to be on it, it seemed like the right thing to do. Do you understand?"

I nodded.

What I understood was that—for some reason known only to God—I had been chosen to be the exception to the rule once again.

Why, Lord, why my brain? I thought.

CHAPTER NINE:
Mishaps and Miracles

God dispatched several "angels" to help my brother through the aftereffects of his stroke.

My mother served as Chad's everyday angel, helping him with tasks that an impaired right hand made much more difficult. Mom managed to be there every afternoon to help Chad write the answers to his homework—literally serving as the "ghost publisher" who enabled his ideas to become legible.

Then there was Chad's physical therapist, who gave him not just exercises, but hope and motivation as well. She made him believe that he could fully recover control of his right arm and leg, and so he worked hard enough to make progress a reality. In fact, by the time the summer of 1990 arrived, Chad was back at the frog pond. A two-handed task, frog catching was the ultimate test of his right hand's ability to coordinate movements with his left.

Early one July morning, as the dew droplets on my grandfather's lawn surrendered to the intense summer sun, Chad, Jimmy, David and I strolled down to the pond. Chad boldly ripped off his sneakers and plunged into the knee-high muck at the bottom. For a few moments, he surveyed the surroundings, his head tracking like a radar disk locked onto its target.

Then, suddenly, he leaned forward, both hands extending in unison—both hitting the water's surface simultaneously. A moment later, he lifted a huge bullfrog from the pond. He displayed it like a winner's trophy.

"Yes," Jimmy, David and I cheered in unison.

Chad smiled broadly. "I still got it," he said with obvious satisfaction.

Another angel who made a difference in Chad's recovery from that stroke was a man named John Jenkins. A motivational speaker and one of only a handful of long-term African-American residents in Lewiston-Auburn, he was enthusiastic about accepting Chad into his beginning karate class, particularly after Doctor McFaul switched Chad from Coumadin to a daily dose of aspirin. Aware of Chad's medical history, John was able to preserve Chad's ego by somehow making the class members feel as though everyone received equal treatment, while actually ensuring that Chad's Fontan heart wasn't overtaxed.

Chad loved John for helping him feel like a normal, healthy boy at a critical time. For reasons that weren't obvious, but that probably had something to do with the early signs of puberty, my brother's body seemed to be weakening again.

Although his heart beat at a normal rate and his breathing wasn't overly labored, he was often ill with infections. Since he wasn't thrilled with his classes at school, he'd never tell his teachers how he was feeling, but instead developed a friendship with the school nurse, another angel whom my mother counted on to watch over him.

Although he had neither medical nor parental training, Brian gradually developed into an important angel in Chad's life. It started way back when Mom and Brian began dating. I remember one particularly crucial conversation between Chad and Brian, during which Chad spoke exclusively about our father.

"My dad's a great soccer player. He led all scorers at

Saint Dom's," Chad said.

"Wow, you must be proud of him," Brian answered.

"Yup. And it was Dad who taught me how to play pool too."

"You're a heck of a good player, so he must be super," Brian said.

"Yup, he is," Chad said.

Occurring on the way to the hardware store in Brian's Jeep and without my mother present, the conversation continued along those lines for almost twenty minutes. I think Chad needed to do two things that day. First, he needed to publicly reaffirm his bond with our dad. Second, he had to test the waters of friendship, see if he could trust Brian to allow him to openly express the genuine love he felt for our father, despite the fact that Brian had witnessed episodes of Chad's hurt and frustration when my father would arrive late to pick him up for custody weekends.

I recall one instance when my father called to tell us he had to work late. In the background, I could hear the sound of a jukebox, the clinking of glasses and the din of background conversation. In bitter frustration, I handed the phone to Chad.

"Okay, Dad, I'll be here. Come over and get me when you can," he said. "See you later."

I glared at my brother as he hung up the phone, because I was angry that he'd let my father get away with lying to us.

"I know he's lying to me," Chad said, calmly. "But he needs me. I have to be there for him."

Essentially, Brian gave Chad the leeway he needed to maintain a bond that only Chad himself was capable of sustaining. While I did my best to avoid my father, scheduling activities with friends during my custody weekends, Chad would make sure he kept my dad in touch with events in both our lives, by spending as much phone or in-person time with him as he could. By contrast to the physical situation, it was Chad who had the stronger emotional heart, who became my father's life support for several years. My uncles have expressed it by observing that Chad was his father's savior. In that sense, my brother's relationship with my father was and is one of miraculous proportions.

♥ ♥ ♥

An organization of angels, the Make-a-Wish Foundation funded an all-expenses-paid trip to Disney World in December of 1990. It was our first encounter with the Magic Kingdom.

Given Chad's name by an unidentified source in Boston, the Foundation's representatives had approached my mother just after the Fontan surgery in the fall of 1989. But Mom was skeptical; she wanted to be sure that Chad continued with his physical therapy before committing to any long trips, and she wanted to learn more about the organization. By visiting us several times that winter, they made Mom feel much more comfortable about accepting their charity, something that never came easily to her. The trip was scheduled for the week after Thanksgiving, 1990.

It was an unforgettable experience. We were picked up by a limo, and during the ride to Portland Airport, presented with five hundred dollars spending money that we had no idea was included in the package.

At Orlando Airport, we were escorted by a Foundation representative, a woman named Chris, who seemed intent on showering us with every possible amenity. "I think you'll need a car while you're down here, won't you?" she said.

"It's not absolutely necessary; I'm sure we can take buses," Mom said.

"No, no, you should definitely have a car," Chris insisted. "What kind would you like?"

"We're not fussy. Something small and economical will do just fine," Mom said, still resisting the temptation to be extravagant.

Chris winked at the rental car agent.

"How about a candy-apple-red convertible, then," the agent said.

"Yeah, Mom, go for it," Chad said.

"Too cool," I added.

"It's all part of the package, Mrs. Boily," Chris assured my mother.

The stylish car was only the beginning. Together with families of other sick children, we stayed at a perfectly manicured complex of garden apartments with Disney-character street names, huge comfortable beds and refrigerators crammed with fruit, ice cream and other goodies.

Every sick child was given an identifying badge that was recognized by all employees of the Magic Kingdom and surrounding businesses. For example, when Chad was spotted at the end of a long line waiting for tables at the *Hard Rock Cafe*, an employee immediately walked back to fetch us.

"Waiting lines don't exist for y'all," the young woman said. Ten minutes later, we were seated at our table and informed that we could order anything on the menu—on the house.

We returned from that wonderful trip in high spirits, cruising along on the notion that good things were beginning to happen to Chad, things that would start to compensate him for the battles he had already waged during his brief lifetime. And as my brother approached the transition to high school, there *were* several other factors that reinforced that optimism. Although still smaller than average, his body had grown somewhat, and he had earned his yellow belt in karate, proving to himself and to everyone else that he'd recovered from his 1989 stroke. In addition, we caught glimpses of emotional maturity through the haze of his emerging masculinity. For example, when Mom sent Chad to a Y.M.C.A. day camp, the staff recognized his interpersonal skills by asking him to become a leader-in-training.

Just when it seemed that our lives were threatening to become more normal, poor Chad was leveled by the blow that—because of its timing and prolonged aftereffects—was worse than any he had so far endured. It was the ultimate reality check for us all.

It began with a Red Sox game. Jimmy had never been to one, and Chad had always been a fan-from-a-distance. So, when two tickets became available, they prepared to head down to Boston in Jim's car.

There was both excitement and apprehension in Jim's body language. People from Maine were universally critical of the perils of the big city and its notoriously insane drivers, and one of our uncles—who daily commuted into Boston—reinforced the negative psychology with some first-hand horror stories.

Jim knew only one route in and out of the city, the one that led to the Longwood Medical area. Fortunately, Fenway Park was located along that route—about a mile short of Children's Hospital—and they made it there with only the typical array of close calls.

Although he'd reached the summer between his sophomore and junior years of college, Jim was still a bit naive when it came to the big city. "How much to park here?" he asked the attendant at a lot on Brookline Avenue, a block from the ballpark.

"Special price—fifteen bucks . . . leave the keys," the attendant replied.

"No way," Jim said, "Keys stay with me." It was an aging, high-mileage V.W., but at the time, it was his prized possession.

"No keys, no parking," the attendant insisted. He pointed up the street. "Same no matter where you park."

"Looks like we're walking home," Jim quipped to Chad as they headed for the ballpark.

The day was clear and warm, and for the first few innings, Jim and Chad gobbled Fenway Franks and basked in the pleasant June sunshine. But as the game progressed, an ominous bank of clouds rolled in off the ocean, bringing a chilling mist to the air and an uncharacteristic barrage of complaints from my brother.

"Jimmy, my stomach hurts."

"Geez, the hot dogs weren't that bad," Jimmy said.

Clutching at his midsection, Chad grimaced in pain. "No, I'm not kidding, it really hurts."

Although he suspected a simple stomach ache, Jimmy wasn't about to take any chances that there was something happening with Chad's heart. He pointed toward the hospital area. "You want me to take you over to Children's?"

Chad shook his head. "Jimmy . . . it's not my heart, it's my stomach." He indicated his extreme lower abdomen. It's weird . . . way down here. I think we better go home."

Despite Chad's reassurances, Jimmy made the entire drive home with his own heart racing and stomach churning, while Chad's complaints about his severe pain escalated. By the time they arrived, Chad's breathing was shallow and labored.

"Oh no . . . Chad . . . what's wrong? Is it your heart?" I asked, greeting them at the door.

"Amy, where's Mom?" Chad asked.

"Upstairs," I said, looking to Jim for reassurance.

"He's sure it's his stomach, not his heart," Jim said.

I pointed at my brother's chest. "Then why's he breathing like that?"

"Because it hurts too much to breathe deep," Chad groaned.

My mother's rush of frantic anxiety was quelled when Chad charged into the bathroom and vomited.

"I think it must've been the hot dogs," Jimmy said, and Mom cooled down another notch.

Unfortunately the pain and intermittent vomiting continued, and just after dawn, Mom and I took Chad to the C.M.M.C. emergency room.

The staff diagnosed acute appendicitis, which considering the range of possibilities, still came as a relief.

"The appendix is swollen and could burst at any moment," a resident told us. I'll have to schedule him for emergency surgery.

"He's a heart patient . . . on daily aspirin," my mom blurted out reflexively.

They didn't seem concerned, behaving as if they were confident that this was a relatively simple problem compared to the panoply of pathology that had characterized my brother's life. "Two or three days and he'll be fine," a surgical resident opined.

The way things had been going, even two or three days was going to be a strain on both my brother's patience and our meager bank account. My father's health insurance had picked up eighty percent of most of the enormous medical costs of the Fontan surgery, but twenty percent of that bill was still a quite formidable sum. And with Chad's stroke coming just three months later, the totals kept piling up.

"Amy, can you stay with Chad for a few minutes," my

mother said to me. "I'd better phone Augusta." Mom was referring to the Maine Department of Human Services, Division of Handicapped Children, whose financial help with items not covered by insurance had been a blessing.

Three days became four and four stretched into six, the physicians explaining that Chad's healing process was slower than would have been anticipated for someone with a completely normal circulation.

The day of his discharge finally arrived, and Chad was animated as he, Mom and I played cards on the table beside his bed.

"Mom, you'd better be here early tomorrow morning to pick me up," Chad said twice. "Mom, I want outta here *early*."

"I'll be here around nine, honey," Mom said.

"Not early enough, Mom. If I don't see you earlier, I'll be phoning home, E.T."

"Very cute, Chad," Mom said. "But I can't be here *too* early, because we have to wait for the doctors to get here, so they can discharge you."

"Don't worry, Mom . . . I'll make them do the discharge stuff early. Just be here, okay?"

The following morning, Mom and I awakened to the phone ringing. It was barely six a.m.

Chuckling, Mom turned to me with eyes sparkling. "That little shit, he's pulling a typical Chad," she said.

Mom picked up the receiver and positioned it so we could both listen. "Chad?" she said.

"No, Mrs. Boily," a female voice answered. "But this *is about* Chad. "This is his nurse. He's started to feel quite ill in the last few hours, and he's been asking for you. We think you should come right over."

As Mom hung up the phone, she looked completely lost. Her sparkling eyes had turned dull, her smile had decayed into another one of those concerned "Oh Lord, what now?" grimaces. She phoned my grandmother, then Brian, in each case, babbling that she knew something terrible had happened, but she couldn't tell them exactly what.

When we arrived at the hospital, Chad's face was fixed into the rigid zombie-like mask that we remembered so well. Tears were pouring down his cheeks.

A half-hour later, after confirming that my brother's left side was flaccid and his speech impaired, they wheeled him down for a C.T. scan. I had never before seen him terrified of a medical procedure, but this time, his face was collapsed into a definite look of despair. The usual bravado, the "I'm used to this crap" smile was notably absent. It was as though something inside was telling him that the stakes had escalated, that being thought of as a crippled child in the eyes of the State of Maine was far different than actually *being* crippled.

As we waited for the C.T. results, my mother told me the story of how she had comforted the limbless, parentless, hydrocephalic baby in the I.C.U. after Chad's infant surgery; how she had thanked God that Chad had the defects he did rather than being a total cripple like the other child. For the first time, I sensed a trembling in the foundations of my mother's faith—as though she were questioning why God would take us so far and then let this happen. It made me realize how much we all depended on her and took her unwavering courage for granted.

"Mrs. Boily, I'm Doctor LeBlanc. We've ordered an ambulance to take Chad to M.M.C.," a young neurologist said, bursting into the Radiology waiting room.

My mother's face furrowed far beyond its years. "Is he in that much danger?" she asked. She threw an arm around me as I started to sob.

"No, he's in no immediate danger," Doctor LeBlanc

said. "All his symptoms point to his having had another stroke, but the only thing we can find on the C.T. is the remnants of the one he had in 1989. He needs to have an M.R.I., and that can only be done in Portland. I've already spoken to Doctors McFaul and Rioux. They'll be ready for him when you get there."

I started breathing again.

"Isn't there something you can do?" Mom asked

"We've started him on heparin . . . it's standard procedure to protect against further damage."

I have never seen my brother so depressed as on the journey from radiology back to his second floor room. The dingy brown corridors and the single room in a non-critical care unit should have looked good to him, denoting that his heart was functioning suitably. But every time he tried to speak to us, a jumble of muffled sounds was the only result. Tears flooded the corners of his eyes and rolled freely down his cheeks. Chad obviously realized that this was worse than anything he'd ever had to cope with. He was nearly catatonic during the ambulance ride to Portland. When they inserted the breathing tube, I noticed that he showed no gag reflex.

"It's just temporary, Chad," I assured him, despite having no reliable information that I was being truthful. At that moment, I would have said anything to ease his pain.

Brian arrived at M.M.C. just as my mother and I were escorted into a conference room. About twenty office chairs were arrayed around a huge oval oak table, at the head of which was a chalkboard and an overhead projector.

At least ten of the chairs were occupied by men and women in either green scrubs or long white coats, Doctors McFaul and Rioux at the positions of prominence near the head of the table. It looked like an entire team of physicians had been assembled to inform us about Chad's condition.

As we took our seats, my mother and I shuddered. Sitting between us, Brian took each of our hands and squeezed.

"Doctor Rioux has the results of Chad's M.R.I.," Doctor McFaul said. "I'll let him explain what they mean."

"As you know by now, Chad's had another stroke," Doctor Rioux said. "The M.R.I. shows that an important brain artery known as the Basilar is blocked almost completely. Not only is there a clot, but the artery itself appears calcified—as though it's sustained gradual wear-and-tear damage."

"What could cause that?" Brian asked.

"There are a number of possibilities we need to look into," Doctor McFaul said. "To begin with, I've ordered an arteriogram for tomorrow morning. It will give us a better idea of what's occurring in the blood circulation in and around Chad's brain."

"What about his left arm and leg . . . and his speech?" my mother asked, voice quavering.

A barrel-chested man with full salt-and-pepper beard, Doctor Rioux stood next to the chalkboard and began drawing x's on what I recognized as an outline of the human brain. "The stroke has caused damage to an area of the lower brain . . . called the pons," Doctor Rioux continued. It's a place where many nerve fibers that control muscle movement pass through to carry information to lower levels of the nervous system. Chad's suffered right-side damage, but since most of these nerve fibers cross over, we're seeing problems on the left side.

"And the speech?" Brian asked.

"Is also a muscular problem. The good news is that we don't see any damage to the higher speech areas of his brain." Doctor Rioux placed another mark on the blackboard. "The speech should return with time."

"How much time?" Mom asked plaintively. "My son

is scared to death that he can't talk."

"Doctor McFaul reached across the corner of the table and placed his hand on my mother's arm. "It's difficult to say, Mrs. Boily. Before we can fully assess his condition, we need to prevent any more blockages from forming . . . to prevent additional brain damage."

Additional brain damage—the words tore through me like rotating fan blades. My mother asked the question that was on all our minds.

"I've heard of people having arteries cleaned out before. Can't you operate on him to clear the block?"

"You're thinking of carotid *angioplasty* . . . where the blockage occurs in the neck," Doctor McFaul said. "This clot is much higher up . . . and it appears fairly extensive. There's hardly any room for blood to flow. Even if we could get at it safely, there's a very strong possibility that part of it would travel into an artery even farther up . . . where it could cause much greater damage, and where we'd never be able to remove it."

Mom jumped out of her chair, her bloodshot eyes wide open for the first time in weeks, her bloodless fingers clenched into tight fists. "This can't be . . . can't be . . . there must be something you can do."

"I'm truly sorry, Mrs. Boily, but other than heparin and more tests, there's really nothing we can do," Doctor McFaul said, as Brian rose to comfort my mother. "You should also be aware that Chad's emotions will seem extreme. He'll likely cry one moment and laugh hysterically the next . . . often for no apparent reason."

We behaved like a procession of robots as we walked out of that conference room, each of our bodies rigid with tension from the shock of what we'd just heard. Up to now, there had always been *some* medical answer, something they could do to help my brother. After thirteen years as a laboratory rat, the experimenters had suddenly abandoned Chad. It was as though they were telling us that his body was too worn down by the ordeal to be useful to them any more. As someone beginning the college application process and aspiring to a career in pharmacy, I knew that my judgment was overly harsh, but my brother's plight was so dire that either tears or anger seemed the only possible emotional outlets, and I didn't want to add to Chad's misery by bawling in front of him.

My mother detoured to a stairwell on the way back to Chad's room. "Amy, please go keep Chad company. I'm going downstairs to call Bob . . . and Ann . . . to see if they can explain this stuff about the Ba . . . what was the name of that artery?"

"Basilar," Brian said.

As I approached the door to his room, my choice of anger over tears was reinforced by the muscular figure of my Uncle David leaving Chad's room, wiping puddles of moisture from his lower eyelids.

"I can't stand how depressed he looks when he tries to talk," David said, embracing me. "He needed to pee, and he pointed to the pee bottle and started bawling. I had to get out of there before I broke down completely in front of him. Mom and Dad are in there trying to cheer him up."

"How does he look?"

"Terrible," David said. "Like all the muscles in his face are frozen. And he hardly moves his eyes."

When I opened the door, Chad almost immediately began to laugh; not his normal contagious good humor, but macabre, like a witch's cackle.

The zombie-like mask and the extreme emotional shifts continued for several weeks. As other members of the family drifted in, my mother had to take each aside and prepare them for what they would encounter beyond the door to

Chad's room. Knowing how important Jimmy's support was to Chad, Mom intercepted him in the hallway when he arrived from his summer job that first afternoon.

"Jim, he can't control his emotions and he can't talk." He'll probably start crying when he sees you," Mom cautioned. "I think the more we can all hold it together, the better it will be for him. He needs all our strength right now."

Although he nodded in agreement, I could tell that Jimmy was stunned, and tensing his jaw, he fabricated a smile—with great difficulty—before slowly making his way into the room.

The worst part of that first evening was my father's arrival. Mom and Brian were telling Chad about the arteriogram; that it would tell the doctors a lot more; that they didn't want to jump into any treatment until they thoroughly checked him out. Despite the circumstances, there was quite a bit of positive energy flowing, as we all somehow tried to inject belief into what we were telling my brother—that things would work out as they always did; that God loved him, and he was going to be all right.

At that moment, my father burst into the room, and within seconds, he began bawling. My father loved Chad so much, and after finally seeing him with a stronger heart, he'd convinced himself, as we all had, that his problems might be over for a while. The shock of realizing the naiveté of that assumption drove my father to desperation.

As I held my father's hand, I saw Brian make eye contact with David and nod toward the hallway. The two of them left Chad's room within seconds of each other.

When David returned, he walked over to the bed and grabbed my father by the arm. "Amos, how 'bout we take a walk down the street for few minutes," I heard David whisper to my father. "I'm really thirsty; buy you a beer."

"Go ahead, Dad," I said. "They said there's too many people in here anyway. Memé and Pepé will be gone when you get back."

My father leaned over to hug and kiss Chad. "Hang in there, bum; I'll be back in a few minutes," he said.

My brother moved his lips as though he was about to attempt to speak, but eyes filled with tears, he settled for a slight nod of his head.

Brian imposed upon David, because at the time, he was well aware of the animosity my father held toward him, despite the fact that Brian and Mom hadn't started dating until after the divorce. Misplaced though it was, Dad's anger made it virtually impossible for him and Brian to communicate as two men deeply concerned about Chad's future.

♥ ♥ ♥

The following morning, I arrived to find my brother's room empty of its patient and occupied instead by a prayer group whose core consisted of my mother, grandmother and Aunts Pat and Claire, with the periodic addition of others such as my Aunt Ann and my grandmother's sisters. While they awaited the results of Chad's arteriogram, they prayed aloud and unabashedly for a miracle.

As they had the prior morning, the team of physicians gathered in the large conference room to report to Mom, Dad, Brian and myself. At first, we were assailed with more bad news. According to the test, Chad was likely suffering from what Doctor McFaul called "Subclavian Steal Syndrome." It had probably developed as a long-term consequence of all the surgeries, beginning with the one to repair the kink in his aorta during infancy. Now, Chad's left Subclavian artery—feeding blood from his heart to his left arm was stealing blood from a nearby artery, the left Vertebral, one that was supposed to be delivering blood to the brain. The steal was so efficient that blood actually moved backward in the left Vertebral Artery—from the brain toward the heart! As I listened, I sat there in awe at just how much of an experiment my brother's body actually was.

Since the Vertebral normally emptied its blood into the Basilar Artery, it was assumed that the wear-and-tear damage in the Basilar—together with the clot currently blocking its blood flow—had probably been a long-term consequence of the steal.

"Unbelievable . . . this is even worse for his brain, isn't it," my mom said, realizing the implications of blood meant for Chad's brain going to his arm instead.

Doctor McFaul nodded. "Yes, if left uncorrected." He pointed to a thin, tan-skinned physician to his right. "But Doctor Paolini informs us that this can be corrected by surgically banding the subclavian to cut down on the amount of blood going to the arm and ligating—opening up—the Vertebral to increase blood flow to the Basilar and brain."

Brian asked the question that was teetering at the edge of my thoughts: "What good will that do if when the blood in the Vertebral gets up to the brain, it's still blocked from going any further by the clot in the Basilar?"

Mom had already informed Doctor McFaul that she had trouble communicating with Doctor Rioux, so it was Doctor McFaul himself who indirectly fielded the question. He rose from his chair and spoke a few words into the ear of a young radiologist, an assistant of Doctor Rioux's. The young physician held up a film of some kind. Mostly black, it was crisscrossed by bright lines that we learned were images of brain arteries.

The young doctor pointed to one of the brighter spots on the film. "The brainstem looks good," he said, his face breaking into a smile.

"What do you mean it looks good?" my mom sputtered.

"The Basilar's clear . . . so are the arteries around it."

"How can it be clear?" Mom asked. "Yesterday you told us surgery was impossible."

The radiologist shrugged. "Well," he said softly, "it's clear."

I was never a believer in overt, God's-direct-intervention miracles, but what the radiologist failed to add is that there simply was no other explanation for the disappearance of the clot in Chad's Basilar Artery. Certainly, his body had the self-healing capacity to dissolve that clot over a span of months or years—everyone's body does—but this clot had disappeared over the course of two days. Whatever prayers the women in the family powered up to heaven, they were strong enough to convince God that a miracle was in order. Even the biggest skeptics—such as myself—couldn't deny that what we had witnessed was something quite remarkable.

Unfortunately, the turmoil was far from over. Initially in agreement about Chad's problem, the surgical team began to disintegrate once his blood flow was unexpectedly restored. The surgeon seemed to interpret the miracle as a sign that the blood steal was not as severe as initially supposed, and he refused to attempt the delicate, risky surgery under the circumstances. Doctor McFaul finally found a surgeon who agreed with his assessment that the surgery was necessary. But between delays in providing diagnostic information and difficulties coordinating the surgeon's schedule with operating room availability, the surgery was postponed at least three times over the course of a week. Plus, the surgeon had the bedside manner of a bedpan, and it was only his wonderfully empathic nurse, Laurie, who saved him from being assaulted by several of the men in my family.

The last postponement drove Mom to the limit of her tolerance for protecting Chad from further psychological harm. "This is ridiculous," she said to Doctor McFaul. "You're taking a child who's trying to cope with the aftereffects of a stroke and subjecting him to even more stress. I'm getting him out of here. Call us when someone's prepared to do the surgery . . . when he can be treated like a person, not a yo-yo."

As Mom began to collect Chad's things, Doctor McFaul gingerly touched her arm. "I agree with your decision, Mrs. Boily, and I apologize for the foul-up. Have him back tonight by eight, and I promise we'll get the surgery done right away."

We took Chad to my grandparents' camp where he spent a relaxing day in the sun while my mother rushed home to bake five cakes that she had promised for that weekend. We returned Chad to the hospital at exactly eight p.m., and the surgery occurred the following morning.

The episode was not without its casualties. Although her faith was restored by the miracle, my mother's threshold for witnessing her son's suffering had been significantly lowered. As we sat in Chad's room awaiting the outcome of the corrective vascular surgery, she whispered words that I never thought I'd hear from her mouth: "He should never have to go through anything like this again. If it ever happens again, I pray God will take him."

CHAPTER TEN:
Tormentors

Gimping along on my left leg, I finally showed up at Y.M.C.A. Camp at the end of August of 1993.

"What the heck happened to you?" one of the counselors asked.

"You wouldn't believe it if I told you," I said.

But the counselors at that camp were awesome dudes. They had never treated me like Danny Dweeb, and I figured I could be straight with them. So after working hard at therapy to teach myself to talk again, I decided to fill them in on my lost summer. I wasn't looking for sympathy. My story was kind of an apology for letting them down by promising to be there and then making like the invisible dude.

"Stuff just kept happening . . . one thing after the other," I said. "Just when I thought they'd let me out 'cause I could walk okay . . . the pain started in my belly. Thought I'd be in the hospital forever."

"You gotta be kiddin' me," a counselor named Lou said. "After all that . . . I mean, the stroke and the artery surgery . . . you had a kidney stone too? Did they have to do more surgery?"

I shook my head. "They gave me pain killers 'till I passed it. God, did it hurt."

I was used to pain; had no choice but to deal with it for most of my life. But passing that kidney stone felt like there was a blistering-hot golf ball stuck in my back, which I then had to pee out of my body. I'd never felt pain that hard-core. Sure, I understood that my Fontan heart was doing its job. And I also knew that the surgery was zipping more blood to my brain. But that kidney stone pain screwed-up my head, big-time. "Am I gonna die?" I had asked Doctor McFaul at one really painful moment. It felt like my body was finally giving up.

"Not if I can help it, Chad," he had said. "Except for this stone, you're actually in pretty good shape, buddy."

Doctor Hourihan—Doctor McFaul's cardiology associate—wrote the same opinion in a chart note. But I couldn't have agreed with them less. They were concentrating on my heart and blood vessels. I was bent out of shape about my arm and leg. In my mind, the whole deal with the Fontan surgery had been to give me a shot at a more normal life. Instead I had ended up with a leg that I often felt I was dragging around, and an arm that felt like it belonged on a little kid's rag doll. The end of that summer was the first time I really understood what it was like to feel sorry for myself.

It was a bad time to be beginning my adolescent growth spurt. I was bored by the eighth grade and definitely ready to split the elementary-school scene. But the thought of becoming a *dweeb* high school freshman with a bum arm and leg made me feel even worse. My doctors thought that because I was walking better, I was also feeling better. But they didn't have to deal with a hand that had trouble turning on a light switch, and for which buttoning a shirt was a major hassle.

When Mom first told us that Brian was building a new house in Auburn, and that we'd all be moving in with him, I got pretty flipped-out. At least there were some kids I knew at Lewiston High—including my sister, who'd be a senior. But moving to Auburn meant changing school districts, and

I spent most of that winter *spazzing* about starting as a freshman in a high school where I had no friends; a gimp among total strangers.

If we'd had a major bankroll, I could have followed in the footsteps of my dad and most of my mother's family by going to Saint Dom's Catholic, but the money scene at our house was always tighter than Arnold's muscle shirt. Mom refused to accept charity—even from Brian—and she thumbs-downed it when I told her I'd get a job. It made me feel like Captain Air-pockets. But with everything that had happened to my body since the Fontan, I totally understood why Mom was so bent. Those four years from 1989 through 1993 probably zapped her energy even more than they did mine.

In what would prove to be a big mistake, I pressured Mom into letting me attend Lewiston High. Brian's new house ran behind construction schedule and we didn't move out of Lewiston until spring. I was eligible to enroll in the high school for that fall.

God blessed me with a totally awesome summer before that first year of high school. I went back to Y.M.C.A. camp as leader in-training, and my *gimpiness* seemed not to matter to the counselors, who relied on me to guide the younger kids through days filled with activities. Those days never dragged, and I never felt like a dork.

My Uncle Bob also taught me how to play chess that summer, and I really got tuned-in to the game. When Amy told me there was a chess club at the high school, I figured it might be a cool way to make some friends. After all, it only took one good hand to move pieces on the board. And God had spared me from the type of stroke that would have turned me into a drooling L-twelver.

I honestly walked into Lewiston High that fall, full of optimism that I could learn some cool stuff and make some new friends. It was a big change from the low-voltage scene at Holy Cross Elementary School, and I was psyched. Optimism swelled in my chest when I spotted my old friend Denny on the first day of orientation.

"Hey, buddy, it's great to see you," he said, slapping my back. "I heard you had a rough time last year."

"Yeah, but I'm pretty cool, now," I said.

"Great . . . this is gonna be a blast," Denny said. "Football games and dances . . . and look at all these cute girls."

Yeah, I see them, I thought, *but why would they want anything to do with me?*

♥ ♥ ♥

It started on the first day I limped down those hallways.

"Hey gimp," a voice called out, echoed by several others. Sometimes I'd just ignore them, sometimes I'd tell them to shut their faces. But I'd always walk away. With a *weesh* left arm and Coumadin in my blood, I stood a decent risk of bleeding to death from a brain hemorrhage if some incredible hulk decided to kick my butt. After fighting so hard to live for thirteen years, it just didn't make sense to risk my life because of a few prehistoric jerks who had to pick on someone like me to make themselves feel like they had mighty rocks.

Maybe I should have done a disappearing act. But it just wasn't my personality to avoid people. I joined the chess club, worked hard at my courses and generally tried to get to know kids who could string more than two words together. A lot of the kids were out-of-staters whose families had come to Lewiston for Maine's social services. They lived in halfway houses and didn't have any real family life. I couldn't help feeling sorry for them. They kind of had a reason to be ticked-off at life. But I was the one they usually seemed to take it out on.

One day after school, I met my sister in the hallway, wandering toward the exit door we usually used to split the school. Suddenly, I froze and did an about-face.

"What's wrong, Chad?" Amy asked, stranged-out by my moves.

I pointed to a boy at a locker down the hall. "I don't wanna even get near that kid," I said.

"Why not?"

"He's in chess club with me and I was watching a game he was playing. I made a crack about one of his moves. You know . . . like nothing major . . . I just said that wouldn't be a move I'd make. Everybody makes comments like that when they're watching practice games . . . it's part of being in the club. We learn from watching each other play."

Amy shrugged. "So why do you need to avoid him?"

I grimaced. "Because he jumped up and went haywire . . . pushed me up against the wall and stuck his fist in my face . . . told me not to mess around with him." I shook my head. "I don't know why he got so bent-out-of-shape."

"It's probably because you dinged his ego a little," Amy said. She took my arm, and we walked out another exit. I was glad she didn't try to fight my battles for me. I asked her not to blather about it to Mom, either.

Unfortunately, Amy decided to motor-mouth to my Uncle David instead. I guess she was flipped-out that she'd be graduating and I'd be solo at the end of the year.

"You want me to come over to school tomorrow and break the guy's arm, just say the word, buddy," David told me. It was tempting. Dave was lifting at the time, and he was maybe two-fifteen, solid muscle. I could have gotten-off watching the chess-dork dribble in his drawers when he saw my uncle. But it wouldn't have been cool.

"Nah; thanks anyway, I'll be okay," I said to David.

Thankfully, I did have one awesome friend who I knew from elementary school, a major dude who caught-a-chuckle from being around me. Denny was a weight lifter, and every once in a while, he threw his weight around for me.

I remember one time when I was kneeling in front of my locker before class. A kid named Larry—who was always zinging me about my gimpy leg—walked up to me and kicked my butt—really hard. The kick drove my head into my locker, and I almost poked my eye out on a hook.

I did the only thing I could do; checked myself for blood and got up in his face. "Why the heck did you do that?" I said.

"Because I felt like it, gimp," Larry said.

That was such a bogus scene, that I figure God made special arrangements for Larry's boomerang. It happened the next week, when Denny asked me if I wanted to come down to the gym and workout for a while.

"I'm not really supposed to workout hard, but . . . sure . . . I'll tool around with some stuff for my arm and keep you company," I said.

"Cool," Denny said. "You can psych me up to press some extra weight."

I changed into my gym clothes and picked out an empty locker. While I was hanging up my street clothes, Larry showed up in the locker room and walked over to me.

"Whose crap is this in my locker?" he said. "This better not be your crap, punk." He stuck a finger in my face. Then, with his other hand, he pulled a blade from the pocket of his sweatshirt. I knew he was a sick puppy, but until that minute, I didn't realize how much he needed a Prozac burrito.

Just then, like magic, Denny bolted out of the weight room and stepped between us. He grabbed Larry's wrist and twisted hard. "This is my friend, Chad's locker. You got a problem with that?" he said.

The blade clanged on the cement floor. "No, no problem," Larry squeaked. Just to be sure he understood, Denny shoved him hard into the lockers.

With Amy's help, I managed to hush-hush this crap from my mom, because I didn't want to give her something else to worry about. Unfortunately, Amy's tongue got loose after a bad scene in my shop class in the spring of '95. My war with Larry was on again.

"Don't say anything, okay," I said to my sister before leaving to board the school bus home that day.

"You think she's going to miss that?" Amy said, pointing at the white gauze bandage on my left arm.

"I'm gonna tell her I fell in gym," I said.

"That might work today, but you know Mom; she'll notice it's a burn when you change the bandage."

"Maybe it'll heal fast," I said. It was a brick-brainer deluxe. With the bogus circulation in my left arm, even the most minor bruise took a week to heal.

Mom's eyes zeroed-in on the bandage the moment we walked into the kitchen. "Oh my God, Chad, what happened?" she asked.

I was cornered, so I decided to fess-up. "I got burned in shop class," I said.

"He means that another boy burned him," Amy said, trying to encourage me to unload some of my psycho-garbage.

"You mean by accident?" Mom asked.

I shook my head. "I don't know why he did it, Mom. Just to be mean, I guess."

"Somebody burned you *on purpose*?"

I explained it to her: "The class was learning how to loosen frozen bolts by heating them with a blow torch. After I unscrewed the bolt with my partner, this other kid just picked up the hot wrench and shoved it into my arm."

Mom looked shocked, but she did her best to make sense of it all. "Chad, did you say something to this boy that made him angry?"

"I swear, Mom. I just tried to make friends with the kid . . . a couple of days ago. Said 'hi' to him and asked him how it was goin'."

Mom's forehead creased. "Then why would he want to hurt you like that?"

Amy answered Mom's question: "He was probably trying to show those other jerks that he wasn't any friend of Chad's, Mom. That's how screwed-up those bozos are."

As much as my sister's explanation hurt, I knew she was probably right. Larry wanted everybody to know that there was no way he'd ever be friends with a gimp like me.

Naturally, Mom charged into school and got up in the principal's face. They suspended Larry for a week. But instead of making me feel good, it put me in a bind. As soon as Larry got back, I had to always be looking over my shoulder, wondering when he or one of the other bozos would try to get even.

As the spring semester wound-down, Mom and Brian stayed on my case about the situation. They thought I should transfer from Lewiston to Edward Little High School in Auburn.

"If I could get a job, then maybe I'd be more like the other guys," I argued.

"I don't think that's the answer, honey," Mom said.

"This isn't your problem, boss," Brian said. "We both know that getting along with people has always been one of your strong points. And it might be okay if it was still like it was when I was in school. I remember there were some bully types who wanted a piece of me . . . but none of them were carrying. I never even considered the possibility of *dying.*"

"Why don't we try E.L.H.S. next year, honey?" Mom said.

"Aw Mom, it'll be like being a freshman all over again."

"You never know what can happen, Chad," Mom said. "God loves you."

CHAPTER ELEVEN:
Real Friends, Real People

I sometimes wondered how Brian could possibly be attracted to me. He was responsible, energetic, sophisticated and incredibly bright—everything I had always hoped for in a partner. Meanwhile, I was a divorced mom, scraping-by, struggling to make a decent life for my kids and fighting to keep my son alive. Why would he take on such burdens, I wondered.

But Brian kept right on surprising me. Recognizing the spiritual beauty in both my children, he realized, in Chad's case, that the years of emergency-room visits and hospitalizations had turned my son into a people person. In place of the bitterness Chad could have easily developed, he instead turned those experiences into a gift—a gift for getting along with people.

Brian's appreciation for Chad's positive personality made it even harder for him to listen to the horror stories coming from Lewiston High. I'm sure that those stories were part of the reason he decided to finish the basement recreation area of our new home. He wanted to provide a safe, comfortable environment where Chad could feel free to make friends by being his lovable, sociable, interesting self.

At first, it seemed like money well-spent, but when

Brian and I got our first taste of Chad's new friends from Auburn's Edward Little High School, we both began to wonder. At the time, Chad wore his hair long, his musical tastes ran to bands like *Blues Traveler* and *Phish*, and he'd even taken up the harmonica. Suddenly, in place of that familiar rock music, we began to hear frantic electric guitars and barely comprehensible lyrics surging up from the basement.

Chad's sudden flip-flop made us temporarily question his motives. He was someone who had fought his entire life for the right to be different. Why was he now passively absorbing the tastes of his peers? Brian and I tried to rationalize it as part of the conflict he faced at becoming a teenager.

Brian reminded me that Chad's hormone surge was telling his body that he was superman—indestructible. But unlike other boys his age, Chad's life experience was completely at odds with the hormone messages. We couldn't even begin to imagine how hard that conflict must have been for him. While the other boys were living-out those hormonal messages about indestructible bodies, Chad had to hold himself back, because deep down, he knew better.

"How's it going at school, boss?" Brian asked at the end of Chad's first week as a sophomore transfer.

"Okay, boss," Chad said.

"From the music I hear downstairs, it seems like you must be meeting some new kids . . . making new friends?"

"Uh huh . . . I guess so," was all Chad would offer in return.

"Friends of Nate's?" Brian asked, remembering that he'd seen Chad chatting on our street with a neighbor's son and a group of other kids we didn't know.

"Yeah . . . some of them," Chad said.

"How about letting your mom and me meet them,"

Brian said. "You know the room downstairs is meant for you to use to entertain friends . . . as well as for family recreation. Why don't you ask them over to shoot some pool."

"Thanks, boss, I'll think about it," Chad said.

It was a few weeks before Chad followed-up on Brian's offer, and we prepared ourselves for a shock. From what we'd seen around town, we expected a bunch of *grunged-out* aliens with lousy attitudes, the manners of Vikings, and a cloud of smoke hanging over them.

One week night after returning from a workout at the gym, Brian and I got home to find Chad and five of his new friends in the basement. They wore silver chains and black clothing, and they had hair colors ranging from gold to shocking pink. One of them had even dyed a red circle into his dark brown hair. But there was no smoke in the room, no alcohol of any kind, and they seemed to be having a great time just sitting around and talking.

We immediately got the feeling that they were just regular teenagers, not all that different from the kids we had hung around with at their age. Best of all, Chad was smiling, obviously enjoying their company.

Brian decided that there was no reason to be anything but cordial. "Hi, I'm Brian," he said. "Welcome to our home."

Several of them stood and extended their hands. "Hi Brian, I'm Max," one of them said. "Thanks for letting us come over. This is an awesome place."

"We really like hangin' out with Chad," another one said, reaching for Brian's hand. "He's one awesome dude."

I smiled. "We sure think so."

We chatted for a few minutes—mostly small talk. With each exchange, our impression that they were decent people grew. There was none of the viciousness or animosity that some of our friends had told us to expect.

"I get the feeling they're okay," Brian said on our way up the stairs.

"I kind of feel that way too. They're respectful and they obviously like Chad," I said.

"Did you see the *Clue* game board? I can't believe they were playing board games. Seems like a throwback."

"I think it's wonderful," I agreed.

Brian turned back toward the basement. "If that's who they really are, I'm going to make sure I let them know that they're always welcome here."

They took his invitation seriously. From that day on, we saw more and more of them, and we gradually met some of their parents. They were nice kids. They rejected tobacco, alcohol and drugs, and consistently engaged in what we considered healthy activities. So what if their addiction was a frantic, up-tempo style of music that we didn't understand. Considering their positive characteristics, they earned the right to get high on what they called "independent music."

Best of all, Chad's new friends were clever where it counted most. They hardly even noticed his weakened left arm; yet, in their own low-key way, they recognized his limitations. Best of all, they slickly found ways to include him in most of their activities. Sometimes it was easy. For instance, when they were traveling to the *Elvis House* in Portsmouth, New Hampshire to cheer-on their favorite bands, Chad was always invited, even though he sometimes couldn't go because of a glitch in his health.

But even when the outing involved physical activity, Chad's friends found a way to include him. I especially remember the Friday evening when the group announced plans for an all-day-Saturday trip to an indoor stunt-bicycle and skateboard park in Portland. As his friends' excitement grew, Brian and I both sensed the darkening of Chad's mood.

Totally aware of the limitations of his arm, leg and thinned blood, Chad understood that jumps, flip turns and curved walls were out of the question for him.

"What's the matter, dude?" one of the boys asked him. "You look like you just ate a peanut-butter pizza."

"Aw, I don't think I'm gonna be able to go," Chad said.

"Why the heck not?" one of the other boys asked.

"Already got plans for tomorrow . . . promised Mom and Brian I'd help clean up around the yard." Chad pointed a finger out the patio doors, toward the yard behind the house.

It was obvious that he was looking for an out—an exit he could slip through without having to set himself up for the kind of ridicule he'd swallowed at Lewiston High. But Brian's intuition told him that this crew was anything but motley when it came to their new friend; that they really did value Chad for himself.

"It's up to you, Chad," Brian said. "We can certainly get by without you tomorrow. There'll still be plenty of yard work to do next weekend."

At that moment, Chad's new friends came up with the gesture that erased any lingering doubts we had about their affection for him.

"Hey . . . know what?" a boy named Colin said; "my dad said I could borrow his videocam tomorrow . . . as long as it was handled by somebody who wasn't gonna drop it because he was on a skateboard."

"What a rush," Steve said. "You mean we could save our stunts and everything . . . the whole day on video?"

"Totally," Colin said. "But we need a designated camera dude. Somebody who'll be steady enough to take the shots and not drop the camera. How 'bout it Chad? Can we talk you into coming as the video man?"

"Videoman, videoman, don't be geeky, say that you can . . . handle that cam," another voice called out.

Chad's grin exploded into a belly laugh.

Not only did this group of teenagers find a way to include Chad, but in the end, they managed to make him the center of attention. The next day, all stunts were performed for the camera—for Chad. He was the man toward whom everyone else's attention was directed. It was a completely new experience for him.

That evening, the group returned to our home chattering and slapping high-fives, but no one was laughing harder than Chad.

"Somebody had a good time, today," I said, as I dished out brownies and frozen yogurt for the skateboard warriors.

"It was totally awesome, Mom," Chad said. "You gotta see some of the great shots I got."

Brian set up the camera to play back through his large-screen video monitor. Sequence after sequence showed Chad's friends smiling and waving at him as they did their tricks. And it all played-out against the background audio track of Chad's laughter and chatter. Brian didn't ever remember hearing Chad laugh so hard around a group of other kids. The punkers had won us over for good.

♥ ♥ ♥

"You gotta be kiddin' me, Brian," Mike, one of our workout acquaintances said a few days later at the gym.

Brian shook his head. "Why shouldn't I let them hang out at my house? They're Chad's friends."

"I guess I'd better bring you up to date on reality," Mike said. "These kids are useless scum. They have no interests except listening to that crap they call music and dying their hair pink. And people had the nerve to criticize our generation for *long* hair. What a joke."

Brian shrugged. "What do their music and their hair

140

have to do with their values?"

"You mean *valuables*? Like the kind you're going to find missing from your house any day now. It's the reason I'd never let them come around my house," Mike said.

"I'm sure that's true of some kids," Brian said, "but I also know some that wouldn't do that."

"Maybe I'm jaded," Mike suggested.

Brian nodded. "Maybe you are. I have no reason to think that way about this group. They might fall through a window because they're wrestling too hard, but they're not going walk out with my V.C.R. Louise and I have established a solid relationship with them."

Brian later told me that he felt cleansed after his little tirade. He was defending the right of individuals to be accepted for who they were; the same right our generation had protested for; the same right that had been missing from Chad's life during that awful year at Lewiston High.

In terms of his social and family life, Chad's sophomore year seemed like the best of times. He and Brian had come a long way, because Brian had never tried to force their relationship in any particular direction. The payoff was huge. It was around that time when Chad began to refer to Brian as his "step-dad."

What Brian didn't realize at the time was that God had placed him in a position of responsibility greater than any he had ever coped with as a corporate vice-president. He was about to be asked to shoulder the biggest challenge of his life.

CHAPTER TWELVE:
Losing Energy

During the summer of 1995, my son with the crippled left arm managed to hold down his first job—working part-time as a dishwasher at a local restaurant. There were times when Chad's energy seemed to sink, but he always bounced back and had his good days too. It was a summer of celebration: of my parents' fortieth wedding anniversary, of my daughter's successes as a pharmacy student. Brian and I even began to discuss the possibility of exchanging vows. With so many signs that our lives were improving, who could blame us for hoping that Chad's serious medical problems were behind us—at least for a while.

I think my first clue that it was an empty hope came that winter, just after the funeral of my nephew, Jason, who died tragically in an automobile accident over the Christmas Holidays. Since Amy was home for the holiday recess, she and Chad drove to the wake together. Even though Chad and Jason had never been close, I remember watching Chad kneel at the coffin, his hand touching his cousin's for quite a long time as he prayed. Amy later told me that Chad cried for nearly the entire drive home.

"I'm so lucky to be here," Chad sobbed. "I can't believe how lucky I am to be here."

"Stop that, Chad," Amy insisted. "Why are you saying that? God loves you."

"God loved Jason, too, but now he's dead," Chad

persisted. "I'm the one who *should* be dead . . . not Jason."

I think the emotional outburst was Chad's way of reassuring himself about his own life. As his energy started to fade again, he couldn't help but think about the tough battles he'd survived, about all the close calls, all the minor and major miracles that had pulled him back from disaster over the years.

When all else failed, Chad could usually use medical terminology to protect himself from bad news. After fifteen years of cardiology lingo, he had become an expert at sloughing-off the big words and the strange jargon.

That all changed one day, in the spring of 1996. Chad's energy had been very poor for several weeks, and Brian drove him to Portland for an office visit with Doctor McFaul.

When they returned home from that visit, Chad looked stunned, and a veil of concern darkened Brian's expression.

"Colin called to see what you were up to, Chad," I said. "He'd like you to give him a buzz back."

Chad stared out the dining-room window into the woods behind the house. "I don't really feel like talking to anybody right now, Mom."

His answer depressed my mood like the undertow of the bone-chilling ocean along the Maine coast. I knew that for Chad to turn down social contact with one of his new friends meant that something very serious was up.

I struggled for words that would cheer him up. "Why don't you have one of the cookies I made, honey."

"No thanks, Mom; I'm not really hungry," he said.

Brian disappeared into our bedroom and motioned me to follow.

"My God, what's wrong with him?" I whispered, easing the bedroom door closed so Chad wouldn't be able to hear our voices.

"McFaul spoke to him in plain English."

I gasped. "What do you mean . . . what's happening?"

Brian put his arms around me. "McFaul told him that his heart was losing energy. As soon as we got in the car, Chad started repeating the phrase: 'Losing energy . . . losing energy; what does that mean, my heart's losing energy?' he kept saying."

"What did you tell him?"

"I tried to beat around the bush, but he kept pressing me for an answer," Brian said. "It was the first time I ever remember McFaul talking completely plainly with him . . . no medical jargon at all."

I shrugged and shook my head, not sure what Brian was getting at.

"Chad knew that McFaul was telling him something serious, and I couldn't lie to him about it. He saw right through me," Brian said.

I nervously massaged my temples. "So what did you tell him?"

"The truth," Brian said. "I told him: 'it means you're heart's failing . . . which is something you already know has been happening for the past few months . . . but nobody's ever said it plainly to you before.'"

"Oh Lord, this is unbelievable; how can this be happening?" I said. The heartache I was feeling had as much to do with the crumbling of my own illusion as it did with my concern for Chad. I realized that like Chad, I had been dismissing heart failure as something that just couldn't happen to us; not again; not now.

"Are you okay? You're pale as a ghost." Brian's hug tightened. He looked like he was afraid I was cracking up.

"What did Chad say?" I asked.

Brian sat next to me and put his arm around my waist. "He knew what was happening. He said: 'Yeah, you're right; nobody ever said that before. My heart's losing energy.'"

Every day for the next two months, we were reminded of the reality of Chad's statement. He had difficulty going up one flight of stairs. His sentences became shorter because of his need to breathe more often—to gasp for enough air to make sounds.

As if my anxiety over Chad's failing health wasn't enough, I also began to notice troubling changes in Doctor McFaul. He seemed more distracted and less assertive. In his office, I saw signs that other interests were creeping into his life and occupying more of his time. For example, the carvings and bowls on the shelves behind his desk revealed that he had taken up woodworking as a hobby. While part of me understood that a man with such a high-pressure job needed diversions, another part was terrified. I realized that Doctor McFaul was showing signs of burnout.

Then, we learned that Doctor McFaul intended to take a leave of absence. He would travel to Mexico to be married for the third time. We had depended on him for fifteen years. The thought of losing his care in this moment of crisis was gut-wrenching.

During the first few days of August, Chad's symptoms multiplied. On top of his shortness of breath, he also developed soreness in his abdomen, he began to vomit, and his stools became dark and tarry. His color was as pale as it had been since before the Fontan surgery.

After admitting him to M.M.C. on August 6, the physicians discovered that Chad had severe gastritis, probably because of a viral infection. Since he was still on Coumadin, a strong blood thinner, this infection caused him to bleed from his stomach lining. They treated him for the gastric bleeding, and gave him Vasotec and Lasix. This drug combination was designed to take the strain off his heart, by preventing it from having to pump against a greater load. No one had to tell me in so many words: His heart was struggling just to keep him alive, again.

"We need to examine Chad's heart over an extended time period to assess the degree of valve problems, Mrs. Boily," Doctor McFaul said.

I gasped. "Valve problems?"

He nodded. "We're pretty sure that his heart muscle is weaker than it was, but part of the problem may be that his shared A-V valve is regurgitating blood . . . meaning that some blood is leaking in a backward direction rather than being completely pushed forward each time the muscle pumps."

"Are we talking about the possibility of valve surgery?" Brian asked.

Doctor McFaul sighed and shook his head. "That would be an improbable course of action . . . because of the weakness and large, abnormally positioned valve opening in Chad's heart. A very high risk proposition."

"So, what now?" I asked.

"For now, we'll treat Chad with medication and hope for an improvement."

That was it. There was never any mention of other possibilities. Maybe it was Doctor McFaul's preoccupation with his own life that distracted him. We later learned that he had mentioned the possibility of a transplant in a letter to Chad's pediatrician, Doctor Marsh. That letter described the steady deterioration in Chad's heart function and characterized any surgery to replace his failing valve as "a surgical tour de force." But no one ever told Brian and me that they had even considered the transplant option.

As if that wasn't enough, Chad was also diagnosed with a low body temperature due to a deficiency in thyroid hormone. We were referred to an endocrinologist who prescribed a low daily dose of synthetic hormone. After a few days on the drug, Chad appeared at our bedroom door one morning. He looked scared.

"Chad, honey, what's the matter?" I asked.

"Mom, my heart's doin' some strange stuff. Speedin' up and jumpin' around. It's really flippin' me out."

"Oh my God, honey, does it hurt?"

"No, Mom, it's just not beatin' steady . . . it beats, then it jumps around, then it's like it stops completely . . . then, it beats again . . . harder."

"I'll see if I can reach McFaul," Brian said, jumping out of bed.

The thyroid hormone had made things worse, because it created a new symptom in a boy who—for the first time as an adult—was beginning to cope with his own mortality. There's no question that Chad was finally mature enough to know that his condition was life threatening. He was facing a type of fear he'd never known as a child.

The thyroid hormone was discontinued, and Chad was given a Holter monitor to wear over the next week. But it gave the doctors very little new information. It basically told them that his heart was now beating even faster, over ninety times per minute—even when he was resting.

We saw Doctor McFaul for the last time in mid-September. The doctor found that Chad's blood oxygen had decreased from ninety to eighty-three percent saturation, way below the norm of ninety-nine. Despite the faster heartbeat, Chad's heart was accomplishing less and less. Doctor McFaul scheduled a cardiac catheterization for the Eighteenth of September—one that would be performed by his associates in his absence. He ordered Chad to stay home from school and rest in bed as much as possible. It was a dismal way to begin his junior year in high school.

Looking back, I can almost understand why Chad climbed on his skateboard one Friday afternoon before that catheterization. It was a desperate act, like the last insane dive of a Kamikaze pilot in his damaged airplane. At an age when he should have had unlimited energy for school and sports, Chad was told that his heart had almost none left.

When my daughter arrived home for a weekend visit that Friday afternoon, she found her brother sitting on the living room couch with a bloody towel wrapped around his left arm. He looked ashamed rather than in pain.

"Oh my God, Chad, what's wrong . . . what happened?" Amy asked.

"Did somethin' real stupid," he said. "Went skateboarding by myself and took a real bad fall."

He held up the arm to show his sister the deep gash in the forearm from which—because of the blood thinners— blood was gushing into the towel. "Didn't wear any pads."

"For God's sake, why did you do something like that, Chad?" Amy asked as she rushed him to the E.R.

"Don't know. I know it was dumb. Felt like something I hadda do. Guess I just spazzed."

Amy held her temper and took it easy on him. She later told us that she thought Chad felt trapped.

Brian put it more eloquently: "He's frustrated by being quarantined at home and thwarted by a body that refuses to honor his feelings of teenage potency," he said, trying to cool me down.

That skateboarding accident was the last hurrah of Chad's Fontan heart—his last-ditch effort to claim his rights as a teenage boy.

We never did make it to the cardiac catheterization scheduled for Wednesday, September 25. On Saturday morning, the 21st, Chad had another bout of vomiting, and his breathing was as labored as I had ever seen. He struggled for each tiny inhale and complained of chest pains. We rushed him to the M.M.C. emergency room. The paramedics measured his oxygen saturation at a ridiculously low 77 percent, the lowest it had ever been. They sprayed nitroglycerine under his tongue to relieve the chest pain and placed him on oxygen, which raised his saturation to around ninety.

The news was almost all bad, and it was delivered by a Doctor Hamilton in Doctor McFaul's absence. Chad's electrocardiogram showed a problem with his heart's electrical system. The muscle contributed to the heart by his left ventricle wasn't pumping at all. That contributed by the once-powerful right ventricle was barely producing enough push to keep blood circulating around his body. All three valves in his heart seemed to be leaking.

Maybe it was the tension of the crisis situation, or maybe we had become so used to depending on Doctor McFaul that anyone else seemed strange. Either way, I felt completely lost. Every one of Doctor Hamilton's words felt like a barbed arrow tearing at my emotions, draining my resolve to preserve my son's life. And in that moment of weakness, I was forced to focus on the possibility that we were going to lose him. My daughter's expression told me that she was holding the same awful thought. Worst of all, I had never seen anything like the concern I noticed in Chad's eyes. I believe it was the first time he had ever really faced the genuine possibility of his own death.

Brian stood there poker-faced, trying to keep us from collapsing, but ultimately, it was God who sent reinforcements in the person of Doctor Maribeth Hourihan, Doctor McFaul's blond, blue-eyed cardiology associate.

Seeing the hopelessness in my face, Doctor Hourihan took me by the arm and led me into the corridor outside Chad's room in the Special Care Unit. "Mrs. Boily," she said softly; "has anyone spoken to you about the possibility of a transplant."

"No," I said; "I don't really know anything about it.

And I'm really flipping-out about how fast Chad seems to be going downhill."

"Then we need to talk about it," she said softly.

She was as close to an angel as anyone I have ever met. At my moment of greatest desperation, she gave me new hope, a possibility none of us had considered.

Putting an entirely new heart into Chad's body—it was an idea that I had been familiar with since my childhood, when the first human heart transplants had been done. I could remember the name Christian Barnaard. What I couldn't do was evaluate the recent progress that had occurred. Transplantation had become a realistic option for someone whose own heart was failing—especially someone like my son who might possibly have an entire life ahead of him; someone who would lose the chance to ever know who and what he could have been without a transplant.

Doctor Hourihan began the process of filling in the gaps in my knowledge. My sisters Ann and Claire—together with their husbands—kept the ball rolling by encouraging me to see it as a realistic possibility. Sure it was scary, but the alternative—losing my son—was a heck of a lot scarier. And if anybody deserved a new heart, it was someone like Chad, my sisters reminded me.

Doctor Hourihan and my family gave us just enough to encourage us to think seriously about it, without giving so much that we would begin to focus on it as a probable event. For that was neither their decision nor ours. That was up to the network of transplant centers around the world, represented in our little world by Boston's Children's Hospital.

CHAPTER THIRTEEN:
Eight Strikes, You're
Outta Here

At the foot of my bed was a stand with a T.V. and a V.C.R. It was the only friendly looking machine in my room at M.M.C. Above my head, all the video screens were showing either blips or numbers. It looked like the helmsman's control panel from a *Star Wars* battle cruiser. Major mind-boggling.

Most of it, I didn't understand. But there was one monitor telling my doctors and nurses what my blood oxygen saturation was. They kept pointing to that screen and rapping about it. So I figured it had to be a big deal. It went up and down like a possessed elevator in a horror flick. The lower the number got, the faster the nurses hustled across the hallway and into my room. And they always looked flipped-out.

The most bogus thing about the room was that it had no private bathroom, so I had to use a porta-potty. It was basically a little trashcan with a toilet seat made for a five-year-old. A total mind-blower. And for some reason that nobody could figure, every time I felt the urge to go, my oxygen saturation fell off the scale. So there I was, sitting on this dorky-looking crapper, and my nurses come running in. I felt like Pavlov's potty animal. It got to the point where I had to post my mother outside the door to my room as a guard, so she could keep the nurses out by letting them know

I was really okay, that I was only doing my bodily functions. You know, just a simple number two.

Between the pulse oximeter, the electrocardiogram leads and the I.V. lines, I constantly felt like I was strangling in wires and plastic tubing. To the right of my bed was a really important I.V. line that the nurses kept wrapped in aluminum foil. They told me that the drug was light sensitive. It was called Amrinone, and it was bright yellow—as close to the color of pee as you can get.

"That's a really important drug for you right now, Chad," one of my nurses explained; "because it's giving your heart a rest and allowing it to recharge."

"I've heard of scaring the pee *outta* people, but never *into* them," I said. "I don't mind if my hair turns that color, but I don't think I'd look real cool with yellow eyes. 'Cept, maybe in an alien screamer flick."

She smiled. "Don't worry, the color goes away when your liver gets through with it. Besides, we're going to try something new that might help your heart even more. It's called 'Dobutamine'."

"Don't think I need any of that. I'm feelin' pretty mean already. How many sticks they gonna need before they give me the new stuff?" By now, I knew that changing anything always meant taking blood—before, during and after. It was like being a stationary target for mutant mosquitoes.

"I meant to tell you about that," the nurse said. "The doctors want to put an arterial line into your hand."

"A what?"

"It's one big stick that'll save you a lot of little sticks. Once they put it in, they'll be able to get any blood they need from that, without having to stick you again."

"Okay, but I know my Uncle Bob's coming to visit, and he's on call, so I don't wanna miss out on talking to him. Mom said my Aunt Ann might be coming, too."

The truth was that I didn't want to miss out on any visitors. I felt sicker than I ever had, and I needed all the encouragement my family had to give me. But Uncle Bob was a doctor and Aunt Ann was a pharmacist, and between the two of them, I figured we could get some info about what was really happening to me; which drugs might help and which might not.

My body gave them the first answer. The Dobutamine made my heart redline. Then, it started jumping around like a frog *spazzing* from the heat. I got dizzy, and my head felt like somebody was trying to stuff it full of hot heavy metal. It was one of the worst headaches I've ever had.

"Mom, tell 'em I need something for my headache; the pain's unbelievable," I said.

My mother hustled out to the nurse's station and dragged back a nurse with some Tylenol.

"It's the Dobutamine," the nurse said. "Some patients don't tolerate it well. We've already discontinued it." She pointed to the golden-yellow I.V. line: "We're going back to Amrinone."

That drug-induced headache didn't bother me half as much as what happened later that day. Two young, nervous-looking doctors came in with a bunch of silver hardware, needles and tubing, and they began to get ready to insert some kind of valve into one of my arteries. Body piercing was cool, but this stuff was totally out-of-hand.

"Once we do this, you won't have to tolerate any more needle sticks for drawing blood," the shorter, clean-shaven doctor said.

I repeated what I had told the nurse: "Hey, I'm used to getting stuck . . . doesn't really bother me."

"This will be much better," the second, taller, mustached doctor insisted.

"Are you okay, Chad?" the first doctor asked. He

watched me struggle to lift my hand so I could catch the attention of my Uncle Bob, who had just showed up in the hallway outside my room. I wanted to signal Uncle Bob to come in before they sent him away.

"You'll have to wait until we finish before you can see your visitor," the taller doc said.

"But he's on call . . . he's only got two hours . . . and, anyway . . . he's a doctor up in Lewiston."

They nodded to each other and one of them opened the door and called Uncle Bob into the room.

"Doctor Tardif, Saint Mary's Hospital, Lewiston," Uncle Bob said, shaking the hand of the taller doctor.

"We're just going to put in an arterial line while you visit with Chad, Doctor Tardif," the shorter one said.

While Bob asked about my health and tried to lift my spirits, Curley and Shemp started drilling for oil in my left arm. I was in major pain, but I chewed on my lip and kept talking to Bob. We talked about chess, football, his three kids, and anything else he thought would take my mind off the weird body piercing.

"Ow! That one really hurt," I yelled. After brick-braining their try at getting the arterial line in my left arm, they had switched over to my right hand.

"Sorry, just one more stick, and we'll have it set up in this hand."

"Ow, come on; that one hurt even more," I shouted.

Their light-brown scrubs were plastered with huge splotches of sweat, and I could tell they were both really bent-out-of-shape. They seemed almost embarrassed by their *spazz*-job.

The taller one with the mustache nodded to Uncle Bob. "Perhaps you could come back in fifteen minutes, doctor. Then we'll be done, and you can visit with Chad in peace."

"No . . . wait a minute . . . I want Bob to stay," I said.

"It's okay, Chad," Bob said, "I'll go check my answering service . . . and I'll be back before you know it."

I couldn't believe that Bob was splitting, and I really got ticked when the Stooges went back to my right arm for a third try.

"Hey, give me a break or something," I said. "I'm really feelin' hot, and I'm tired of you hurtin' my arm right now."

"But this needs to be done, Chad," the shorter doctor said.

"No it doesn't. I already told you that I never minded the needle sticks, but nobody listened." It was one of the few times I had ever gone *postal* with doctors or nurses. But this was ridiculous—spending time with my uncle was much more important than avoiding a few needle sticks, and no one wanted to listen to my opinion.

"We'll just try one more place, then we'll give you a break," the shorter one said.

"No, just give me a break, now . . . and get my uncle back in here."

"We can't do that . . . but we can give you something for the pain." The taller doctor left my room, returning a few seconds later with some small pills in one of those paper pill cups that double as ketchup holders at *Wendy's*.

The pills got me a little drowsy, but when they started jabbing at one of my ankles, I could still feel the pain through the haze. I did my best to tolerate it, hoping they would get it done and split, so I could have one more rap with Uncle Bob.

They tried and blew-it twice more in each ankle for a total of eight bozos. It had been two hours since Bob first arrived, and two hours was all he really had before he needed to get back to the hospital in Lewiston.

"Okay, that's it; three strikes, you're out . . . you guys

I guess they realized I had lost it, that I wasn't going to take any more. Or maybe they figured that the stress of the whole thing was doing me more harm than good. They collected their stuff and split.

I never got to see Bob again that day. But I did begin to learn a lesson about not always hiding my feelings. It was a lesson I'd need to use soon. Clueless about what else to do for me, Doctor Hourihan transferred me to Boston on September 24.

CHAPTER FOURTEEN:
Getting On the List

Boily, Chad — in room, the receptionist wrote on the status board in the parents' waiting area. I jumped out of my chair and went looking for Brian and Amy, who were catching a few needed minutes of naptime in a room next door. Chad's first set of tests was finished, and I was anxious to find out the results. I was impatient to know whether the cardiologists at Children's Hospital would agree with Doctor Hourihan's assessment of his condition.

The parents' area at Children's was a place of refuge within a wilderness of desperation. A sunny common room overlooking the Boston Skyline was stocked with books and games and had a status board with a line for each child on the unit. The board was used as a message post, with everyone sharing the responsibility of answering the phone and taking messages. We got the feeling that all families were rooting for one another—combining their healing energies and prayers.

The hospital's outreach to families went even further. Brian, Amy and I were able to spend several nights in an old Victorian residence that had been converted into a guesthouse for parents of transplant patients. We were charged only twenty dollars a day for clean comfortable sleeping quarters within walking distance of the hospital.

As welcome as Children's tried to make us feel, we were still unprepared for the discomfort of the medical uncertainty that continued to revolve around Chad. None of us expected either the crash course on organ transplantation or the doubtfulness about Chad's eligibility for a transplant that those days in September of 1996 held in store.

I awoke Amy and Brian, and we headed for Chad's room. On the way, I did my best to wipe the worry from my face. Chad was foundering, and he needed every bit of emotional support we could muster. Most of all, he needed to see his father. I had phoned Amos just before we left for Boston; had pleaded with him to try to be there. My ex-husband had moved to Florida where he had better job opportunities. But God bless him, he promised he would come.

When we reached the nurse's station outside Chad's room, I was grateful to see two familiar faces. Amos and his brother Roger had just arrived. They had come straight to Children's from the airport. They looked tired, but their exhaustion didn't stop them from doing their best to cheer up Chad.

"Hey Chad, great to see you. You auditioning for the movies or impersonating a halogen head lamp?" Roger quipped, as he playfully tousled Chad's platinum-blond punk hairdo.

"Aw, it's a cool color," Chad said, swatting at his uncle's hand.

Amos grimaced. "Yeah, real cool . . . on Madonna . . . maybe."

"Hey Chad, did you hear the one about the priest and the nun in the woods?" Roger asked.

Chad's eyes brightened. "Uh-uh; is it good?"

"I'll let you decide," Roger said. I held my breath, hoping for something clean.

"A priest and a nun were lost in a snowstorm," Roger began. "After a while, they found a small cabin in the woods.

Being exhausted, they prepared to go to sleep. There was a stack of blankets and a sleeping bag on the floor but only one bed. Being a gentleman, the priest said, 'Sister, you sleep on the bed. I'll sleep on the floor in the sleeping bag.'"

"So just as the priest got zipped up in the bag and was beginning to fall asleep, the nun said, 'Father, I'm cold.' So the priest unzipped the sleeping bag, got up, got a blanket and put it on her."

"The blanket, Chad, not his body," Amy said, when she noticed the twinkle in her brother's eye. "God, you're such a pervert, sometimes."

Roger continued: "Anyway, the priest got into the sleeping bag again, zipped it up and started to drift off to sleep. So the nun says 'Father, I'm still very cold.' He unzipped the bag, got up *again*, put another blanket on her and got back into the sleeping bag."

"Just as his eyes closed, she said, 'Father, I'm sooooo cold.' This time, the priest stayed in the bag and said: 'Sister, I have an idea. We're out here in the woods where no one will ever know what happened. Let's pretend we're married.'"

"Who's the pervert, now?" Chad said to Amy.

Roger finished the story: "So the nun said, 'That's fine by me, Father. We'll pretend we're married.' To which the priest yelled out, 'Okay, honey, then get up and get your own freakin' blanket.'"

Chad burst into a silly giggle. But after just a few seconds, he began coughing and gasping for air. He grabbed for the oxygen mask hanging over his head.

The good-natured razzing and the silly jokes helped us all release some tension. Still, I could tell that the same questions were running through everyone's mind: *Was there anything these doctors could do that the ones in Maine couldn't? And if not, was a heart transplant the only possibility*?

Maybe I'd seen too many horror movies. But the vision of surgeons removing my son's heart made me nauseous. Several family members kept reminding me that as scary as the prospect was, it might also be the answer we'd been looking for his whole life. Yet I couldn't put aside my greatest terror: the surgery was all or nothing. If it failed, my son would be gone.

♥ ♥ ♥

Over the next few days, I began to accept the idea that a transplant might be our only option. We saw that the same drugs were having the same minor effects as they had had at M.M.C. The Amrinone helped Chad's heart, but it obviously wasn't the answer because it could only be given I.V., in a hospital. The doctors suggested that the weakening of Chad's heart might be due to a viral infection, but after an echocardiogram, a C.T. scan and a cardiac catheterization, the tests came back negative for that long shot, and the diagnosis stayed the same. Chad's patched-together Fontan heart was simply giving up.

Next, Doctor Keane—Chad's cardiologist from the Fontan surgery—stepped aside, and Doctors Leslie Smoot and Stan Perry—the cardiologists on the transplant team— stepped in. We were fond of Doctor Keane's soft-spoken, encouraging personality, and when he voluntarily took himself off the case, the message was hard to ignore.

Cornering us at the nurse's station outside Chad's room, Doctor Smoot outlined the possibilities. She explained that because of immunological research and new anti-rejection drugs like Cyclosporine, heart donors and recipients only had to be matched in blood type; the tissue-type match that was desirable in liver and kidney transplants wasn't a problem for us. Finding a donor wouldn't be a million-to-one shot. Heart-transplant rejection had become more manageable under less-than-perfect conditions.

Doctor Smoot also presented the down sides. She explained that the donor could be male or female, but had to be between early teens and forty, with no circulatory problems.

"Why forty?" I asked.

"Chad's sixteen, Mrs. Boily," Doctor Smoot said. "To risk the procedure and its immunological consequences, we'd need to know that there was a good chance the heart would last him a lifetime." She paused to smile reassuringly. "There are an enormous number of people in congestive heart failure who are awaiting donors. A healthy forty-five-year-old donor would be appropriate to someone in their sixties, but not for Chad."

"I didn't realize there were so many complications to decide who gets a heart," I said.

Doctor Smoot nodded. "It's a very complicated process that sometimes doesn't seem very fair . . . and it's not even worth progressing beyond the medical aspects until the decision to list Chad is actually made."

"Decision to list!" I said with an edge of hostility. "I thought you already decided that there weren't any alternatives." I could feel my anger burning. After leading us down this road, they were suddenly telling us that it might be closed.

"I don't believe this," Amos grumbled. "He's just a kid; he deserves to live."

Brian put his hand on my arm, and as he usually did, turned the conversation back to the issues. "You mentioned the immunological consequences, Doctor Smoot. Can you elaborate, please?"

"Sure. It's very important to understand that you'd be

trading one set of problems for another. The drugs work very well at suppressing rejection, but as a side effect, they'll make Chad more prone to other types of infections, such as those by viruses. It will be absolutely necessary for him to take extremely good care of himself in every way—nutrition, cleanliness, physical and psychological stress."

"How sure can you be that the anti-rejection drugs are working?" Brian asked.

"We don't take any chances," Doctor Smoot said. "Chad will have to come in for a biopsy—at first, every week—during which Doctor Perry will snip a tiny piece of muscle from the inside of the new heart . . . via catheterization. It's proven to be the earliest indicator. We look microscopically for white blood cells invading the heart muscle."

"Suppose you find them?" I gasped.

"Then we get more aggressive with the drugs to stave-off the rejection process. If things go well, the biopsies get less frequent . . . every month . . . then every two months etcetera."

The most important factor that moved us toward the transplant was Chad himself. As the hours passed in that hospital bed, Chad began to speak up—at least to us.

"Mom, if it could help me feel that much better, then I want them to do it. I don't wanna feel like this anymore," he said.

"Are you sure, Chad? Because, you have to understand that you'd be trading one set of problems for another, honey," I said.

"Don't care, Mom . . . it doesn't scare me. I just don't wanna live like this anymore."

"That's something you need to tell Doctor Smoot, Chad."

"Can't you just tell them? C'mon Mom, I'm like feelin'

164

real crappy right now."

"Chad, I'm sick of this," I said, forcing myself to sound angrier than I was. And I *was* tired of hearing Chad's uninformative responses to his doctors, even though I realized that they were habitual, a result of Chad's lifetime pattern of not complaining.

"This isn't going to work, Chad," I finally said, in frustration. "I know you, but I'm *not* you. *You* have to do this. *You*!"

As a last-ditch try to get Chad to speak for himself, I asked for help from my brother, Jim. Working a new job in Boston allowed Jim to come by every night, and he eventually found a moment when he could be alone with Chad.

My brother knew that he needed to be direct. "Listen Chad, you've gotta talk to the doctors," Jim said. "You've gotta say you want to know what's going on."

Chad shrugged, but before he could make an excuse, Jimmy continued: "They're doing this to *your* body. If you don't ask questions, they're not gonna know what you're thinking. If you're worried about screwing it up yourself, maybe you can at least tell your questions to someone knowledgeable—like Bob or Ann—and have them ask the doctors for you. Is that what you want?"

Chad shook his head.

Jimmy squeezed Chad's hand and hugged him reassuringly. "Then it's time to get it done, buddy. You know we're all behind you. Just tell 'em straight-out."

The next morning, I walked out of Chad's room the moment Doctors Smoot and Perry showed up. I backed away from the door and watched Chad's body language through the glass-paneled wall. Chad looked excited, and when his doctors came out, their expressions had changed. They seemed happier, more satisfied, as if a weight had been lifted from their shoulders. My son had finally made his pitch for a new heart, and he had done it in his own simple terms. He described how he couldn't even walk the hallways at school, and he at least thought he should be able to do that. Without using any fancy words, Chad let them know that his quality of life was horrible.

We next had a long meeting with a social worker, the first of several sessions to tell us about the procedures for listing, transplantation and the post-transplant period. We would not be allowed to know the name of the donor. And only after several months had passed, would we be able to express our gratitude—in writing, with the hospital social services department acting as go-between.

There was still one last step that I needed to take, and I took advantage of the opportunity when we were introduced to Chad's future surgeon. A short, dark man with black hair combed straight back from a pleasant rounded face, Doctor Del Nido had a genuine peacefulness about him.

As I had done with Doctor Nowicki sixteen years before, I took Doctor Del Nido's hands in my own. They were small and soft, and I felt a great comfort flowing through them into mine.

"Looks like we have a big job ahead of us," I said.

He smiled warmly. "Yes, we definitely do. But I feel that it will be fine, because I never do my work alone." He looked out the window of Chad's room and raised his gaze toward the sky. I was filled with serenity. We were ready.

Four days after admission to Children's, I was handed the forms that would place Chad on the transplant list. Before signing for my son, I let him know, one last time, that the decision was his.

"Okay, Chad, you're still under eighteen, so I have to sign for you," I said. "But this is *your* life and *your* decision. Tell me you're absolutely sure before I do this."

"Absolutely, Mom. I want a new life," he said, without

hesitation. "Sign it."

Once the decision was made, they transferred Chad to a regular hospital room for a final evaluation. It was during those few days that we first faced the Catch-22 of transplant listing. From conversations with doctors, nurses and social service staff, we discovered that Chad's position on the transplant list depended on how critical his health was. And any patient who could be discharged from the hospital was automatically considered less critical than one who was still there. It didn't matter that—in or out of the hospital—Chad's heart was still failing. It threw a whole new ingredient into the recipe, one that seemed like it just didn't taste right.

Sensing our depressed mood, Doctor Smoot tried to cheer us up with optimism that the transplant would come about. "Tell you what, Chad," she said. "When you get your heart, I'm going to celebrate by dying my hair the punk color of your choice. How about half red, half green . . . for the Holidays."

"Cool . . . but how about purple," Chad said.

"Not my best color, but purple it is."

Thankfully, Chad seemed to be riding a wave of optimism, concentrating on the possibility that he now had a real shot at feeling better than he ever had before. To someone who had spent an entire life with various types of defective hearts, the idea of finally owning a healthy one was mind-boggling. It was understandable that Chad couldn't help bringing the possibility into almost every conversation.

"Can you tell me what blood type you are, Chad?" a new nurse on the ward asked, in passing.

"Sure can," Chad said. "How 'bout you, can you tell me yours?"

The nurse smiled. "Of course . . . I'm type A positive."

Reaching over to the night table beside his bed, Chad picked up a pair of scissors and waved them at the nurse. "Perfect match," he said, snapping the scissors open and closed. "Can you spare a heart?"

Discharged from Children's on October 5 with pagers and renewed hope, we drove back to Maine to begin what we knew, on the average, could be an eighteen-month wait for a suitable donor. I prayed that there was some plan in the mind of the Almighty for keeping my son alive until that heart became available.

CHAPTER FIFTEEN:
Seventy-two days

Hearing voices outside, I tooled through Brian's office to the front of our house. The second-floor windows overlooked the walkway that led up to the front door from the driveway. The walk looked really cool, because Mom had just planted some baskets of purple mums for the fall. Their color reminded me of Doctor Smoot's promise to dye her hair when I got my heart. Getting a new heart—it was what I thought about most of the time.

Down below, my dad was standing near a boulder that the house builder had left in place at the edge of the walk. Dad was telling Brian about the hassles he'd gone through, trying to find a place to stay near Children's Hospital. Dad and Uncle Roger had first bunked with a friend in Hull, almost an hour south of Boston. They had gotten lost, detoured, and stuck in hard-core Boston traffic jams. Over the last few days of my stay at Children's, they had found temporary digs in an old widow's house near the hospital.

"She was real nice," Dad said to Brian, "but there was only one single bed, so I ended up on the couch."

Brian cringed. "That must've been uncomfortable."

"Not only that," Dad said, "but the old woman wandered around the house . . . like a ghoul . . . in the middle of the night. I hardly got any sleep."

I caught-a-chuckle thinking about Dad in a ghoul's house, but I had to zip my lip so they wouldn't know I was eavesdropping. So I thought back to the first time—a couple of years before—when I'd overheard a conversation between Dad and Brian in that exact same spot. They didn't know I was listening that time, either.

It was just before Dad split for Florida. That short conversation between Dad and Brian was a real brain-bender, a wake-up call for me. It made me realize that both of them loved me a lot.

I remember my father shuffling his feet and staring up at the sky, like there was something major he needed to say, but didn't know how. "I guess I'll see you around," he finally mumbled to Brian.

Looking like his collar was too tight, Brian threw out his hand. "Amos, good luck in Florida; I hope it works out," he said.

As he shook Brian's hand, Dad found a way to say something that I know was very hard for him: "Thanks for taking such good care of Chad, Brian." Without another word, he turned and walked down the driveway.

Now, two years later, they were a little looser with each other, mostly because they were both bent-out-of-shape about my health.

"You think it's really gonna be a year-and-a-half wait?" Dad asked.

"God, I hope not," Brian said. "I don't know if he can make it for eighteen months. It makes me sick to have to say this, but I'm hoping it'll happen over the holidays . . . a lot of car accidents."

Dad nodded. "I'll be here, no matter when it happens."

I couldn't see Brian's face well, but I could tell that he wanted my father to be around when the time came for the transplant.

"Listen, Amos, when you do come up . . . whenever it is . . . why don't you stay in my beach house at Old Orchard,"

Brian said. "Use it as your base of operations. It's a straight shot down Ninety-five to Boston, and there's a room at the hospital you can probably sleep in every so often when you need to stay over."

"Thanks, Brian I really appreciate it," Dad said. He climbed into the car, and he and Uncle Roger left for Portland Airport. I hoped it wouldn't be a year-and-a-half before I'd see him again.

Brian was right. I don't think I could have made it that long, waiting for a new heart. My health was getting worse every day. After just a couple of hours of schoolwork with my home tutor and a rap with my visiting friends, I'd feel totally *weesh*. I had trouble sleeping, and my spirits were really *sub-woofer*. Plus, my blood oxygen saturation kept dropping into the twilight zone. It got so bad that Mom and Brian had to take me back to M.M.C.'s Special Care Unit for an Amrinone recharge every two weeks. The docs had said I'd need a recharge once a month, so twice a month was definitely not cool.

If there was any doubt left in my mind about the transplant being the right way to go, it went south when I met Owen Stacy during one of those recharges in November of '96. I think it was Doctor Hourihan who set it up. She knew that my spirits needed a recharge, too.

Owen's age was either three or sixty-five, depending on when you started counting. "Chad Boily, my name's Owen Stacy the Second," he bellowed, as he walked up to my bed in the Special Care Unit. "And it's darn lucky for you that I'm the one who's here."

"Why?" I asked, looking at him cross-eyed.

"Because, Owen Stacy the First would've never even made it through the front lobby, much less all the way over here to Special Care . . . at least not without a stretcher, two paramedics and a rolling oxygen tank."

"Huh?" I said, shaking my head. He reminded me of my great-grandfather—high-voltage mind and eyes that didn't miss a trick.

"My heart, Chad . . . the old one had no energy left in it. I've been told you have the same problem." Owen said.

"Yup, my heart's losing energy, all right."

"That's a darn shame after just sixteen years. At least I got sixty-two out of mine."

My brick-brain finally shifted into first gear. "You had a transplant at sixty-two?"

"You betcha I did. But I would've have it sooner if I'd known how good it was going to make me feel."

"It really helped you a lot?"

"Like night and day, Chad. I couldn't do anything; now I do whatever I darn please. You needn't be scared, boy. Those surgeons know what they're doing."

"I'm not scared of the operation . . . I'm scared of falling off the list," I said.

"Don't you let 'em rattle you, Chad. I waited a long time for mine . . . then they said I was too old . . . wasn't going to happen. Heck, at least you don't have that working against you."

"I guess not," I said.

"Just hang in there, Chad; keep those spirits up. 'Cause it'll be worth the wait. I guarantee it." He pulled a pen from his shirt pocket and scribbled on a piece of paper. "Just give me a phone call if you need a pep talk, okay? I live right nearby."

"Sure, thanks," I said as Owen waved good-bye and disappeared out the door.

Like night and day; Owen's words stuck in my head. I decided, right there, that no one was going to bully me off that transplant list. If a sixty-two-year-old dude could get charged-up from a new heart, then why couldn't I?

172

But it was more than just "the list" that kept doing a number on my head. It was other stuff, too. Like something I heard from one of the docs, at the end of that recharge visit. I should probably be staying in the hospital, the doc said—just in case there was an emergency that had to be handled right away. After all, there was always the chance I could die before a paramedic team could get me to M.M.C.

The only medicine that really helped was the love that kept coming from my friends and family. For instance, there was the night my friends were going to a concert that my mom knew I really wanted to see.

Since the concert was in Portland, Mom asked my friends if they would stop in to see me. I remember that she and Brian had to be slick to sneak them past the nurses. With all those cool hair colors, they were pretty hard to camouflage.

"Guess what?" my friend Max said, as he squeezed into the small hospital room. "We knew you couldn't make the concert . . . so we figured we'd bring the concert to you." He loaded a CD into my portable player.

Meanwhile, everybody else gathered around my rolling tray table and began pulling pieces of cardboard out of pockets and daypacks. A few minutes later, they rolled the table over to my bed. Those crazy dudes had built me a shoebox stage complete with cardboard musician-dudes.

"Outrageous . . . you guys are awesome," I said. It was one of the coolest things anybody had ever done for me.

♥ ♥ ♥

I'd be lying if I said that the thought of dying didn't scare me a little. But I was almost as flipped-out by the thought of spending whatever was left of my life in a hospital. At least at home I had my music, my family, my stuff, and visits from my great friends. Unfortunately, I was at a point where my heart could go *postal* so fast that in just a couple of hours I'd be gasping for air.

My last recharge came right before Thanksgiving, and it almost made me feel like giving up. They woke me up and asked if I wanted to go home. Naturally, I said "yes," which got me thinking I was being released. They told me to call my Aunt Claire, who was my ride that day.

All of a sudden, the doc came back into my room with a totally new rap: "Why don't you make yourself comfortable and stay for a while," he said.

They seesawed about me for a couple of more hours, and I was getting really ticked. It took a phone call to Boston before they finally made the decision that I could leave. Everybody who saw me afterward could tell that the whole thing was doing a major number on me. It got to the point where my sister told my mom that she wished she could just get it over with by giving me her heart.

"Why'd she say that?" I asked my Uncle David just after we got home from M.M.C.

He gave me a big hug. "Because sometimes you don't know what you've got until you're in danger of losing it. She thinks about you constantly, you know."

"Hey, I feel like crap, but I'm still here," I said. "I just don't wanna live like this anymore."

"You aren't going anywhere, buddy, 'cept back to Children's for the transplant," Dave said.

"Soon," my Aunt Claire said from the doorway to my room. "And we're with you all the way. Don't worry . . . we're all going to be there; I don't care what day it is . . . Christmas Eve, Christmas Day, whatever; we're there."

It was their great faith that kept me going—my family's belief that God had a plan for me; faith that the transplant was part of that plan.

Aunt Claire wasn't that far off. And somehow, Doctor Smoot turned out to be a prophet, too. Her "half-red, half-green for the Holidays" was right-on-the-money. Because on that fateful evening of December 9—just seventy-two days after my transplant listing—a young woman, carrying an organ donor card, gave me a shot at a new life.

CHAPTER SIXTEEN:
On the Eighth Day, God Created the Winds

It was four a.m. on Tuesday, December 10. Brian, Amy and I were huddled together in the parents' waiting area of the Children's Hospital Cardiac Intensive Care Unit, doing our best to keep the conversation from sinking. We were exhausted, but we knew that sleep was out of the question. Chad was down in O.R., and we would continue our vigil of prayer until that new heart was safely beating in his chest.

I wasn't really superstitious, yet I couldn't help trying to reassure myself by focusing on what seemed to be good omens connected with this day. I thought of my ex-husband, who at that moment was braving the frigid December wind outside the hospital, so that he could calm his nerves with a cigarette. Amos had made it up from Florida just in time, grabbing the last seat on the last available flight. It had to be a good sign, I thought. Thinking of Amos also reminded me that we had switched from his insurance coverage for Chad to a more comprehensive plan just two weeks before. Without that improved insurance, there is no way we could have afforded the transplant.

Finally, I allowed myself to dwell on a conversation I had had with a friend in Lewiston. Louie had recently lost his daughter, Stacie, to brain cancer, after a terrible two-year ordeal. Stacie was a close friend of Amy's, and her death had left my daughter in shock, wondering how she could believe in a merciful God, how she could be optimistic about her brother after the tragic loss of her young friend. I decided to remind her of my conversation with Stacie's father.

"It's going to be okay, Amy. I know it is," I said.

"How do you know, Mom?"

"Because I know Stacie helped this to happen. Louie told me that he prayed to her at Mass on Sunday . . . asking her to find a donor for Chad. I'd say the answer came pretty quick, wouldn't you?"

My daughter shrugged. "I guess so, Mom."

"What's the matter, honey?" I asked, sensing a deeper reason for my daughter's concern.

Amy's forehead furrowed. "I'm freaked out by the thought that there'll be a few minutes when Chad won't have a heart, Mom."

A nurse's head appeared in the doorway. "I wanted to let you know that Chad is safely on the bypass machine, and Doctor Del Nido has started the operation," she said.

The nurse's information—coming on the heels of my daughter's fear—opened the door to my own terror. My mind drifted back seven years—to the Fontan surgery and my dread of the bypass machine. As much as I had hated the thought of my child's life maintained by a machine, at least back then I had known that Chad's own heart was still there to take over if needed.

But the transplant surgery gave me a much eerier feeling. It seemed as if the line between life and death was much closer. For some period, maybe a few minutes, maybe longer, there would be no heart inside my son's chest—no heart at all. He would be almost a corpse; missing the amazing organ that kept all his other organs going.

My mind probably cycled back to that gruesome thought at least twenty times during the endless hours of that morning. And when they informed us that the donor heart had arrived from Mass General, my anxiety created another awful possibility. Suppose they turned off the machine and that new organ decided it had had enough, that it really didn't want to start pumping again? Then what?

With Amy out of the room for a few moments, I dumped my anxiety in Brian's lap.

"That's not going to happen, honey," he said. "They've done this hundreds of times. They'd never put the heart in if they didn't think it was healthy." He hugged me tightly and kissed me on the cheek.

He's right, I thought, but the reassurance lasted all of thirty seconds. I knew the answer to my question only too well. If the new heart refused to beat, my son would be dead. I'd never again hear his voice, see his smile, feel his face against mine.

Doctor Stan Perry's tall, slim figure appeared in the doorway shortly after Amos returned from his extended cigarette break. There was a shuffling sound as the four bodies in the room tensed.

"The new heart's in, and it's functioning well," Doctor Perry said. "He's off the bypass machine."

"Oh, thank God," I said, and my short prayer was immediately echoed by the other three voices in the room.

As we exchanged hugs, I felt an exhilaration unlike any I have ever known, nor ever expect to feel again. After sixteen years of swimming hard for survival in a cold angry ocean, the current had suddenly shifted toward shore and become tropically warm and friendly. My son with the courage to survive that choppy water would now be swimming home to us through a placid cove on a bright summer's day.

By the time the next report came, it was already late morning, and many members of my family had arrived. My emotions crashed again, when they told us that Chad's chest was still open. The heart was beating well, but there had been more bleeding than usual, and the surgeons couldn't close until they controlled it. Because of the adjustments made to Chad's circulation during his previous surgeries, Doctor Del Nido had needed to stretch one of the heart's major veins to suture it to Chad's.

Close him up, please, close him up, I thought to myself. *There are germs everywhere; suppose one gets in there and causes an infection.*

In retrospect, I realize that I was being paranoid. He was in a sterile operating room with the best surgical staff under the most carefully controlled conditions. But at the time, my emotions were so discombobulated that no amount of logic was of use to me until I could see my son in his room—touch his warm hand, verify for myself that my Chad was whole.

It was nearly four in the afternoon before Doctor Perry appeared again to bring us up to date.

"Is everything okay, Doctor Perry?" I asked nervously.

"Yup . . . looking good right now," he said, the underarms of his blue scrubs showing several loops of dried perspiration from his undoubtedly hectic day. "Give us about twenty minutes, and you can see him." He smiled, turned in the doorway and disappeared.

Twenty minutes became almost an hour, and the impatience in the room multiplied as each of us longed for the opportunity to see the boy with the new heart. How would he look? What would his mood be? Would he be in pain?

Brian, Amos and I got to go in first, and we were

immediately reminded of the tradeoff of organ transplantation. We had to put on sterile masks and gowns to minimize the risk of carrying bacteria into Chad's room. And poor Amy was told that she'd have to stay outside the room and view her brother through its glass wall with the rest of the family. She had a bad cold, and there was no way Chad could be directly exposed to a virus so soon after his immunosuppressive therapy.

The respirator tube in his windpipe didn't stop Chad from sticking out his tongue at Brian or flinging a bird toward his uncles. We knew right away that his new heart hadn't done much to change his personality.

When he squeezed my hand, I became aware of what was new—fantastically new. For the first time in his life, my son's nail beds were pink. I held up his hand and pointed to his fingernails, mouthing the word "pink" so everyone outside the room could share in my amazement. Through the glass wall, I saw my brother-in-law pointing toward the monitors behind Chad's bed. Ninety-nine percent, the oxygen saturation screen revealed. *My God, my son is normal*, I thought.

Sensing that Chad needed something, the nurse behind us came forward to his bedside, only to discover that Chad was trying to speak.

"We'll take that tube out soon, hon," she said. "But, for now, I'm afraid you'll have to live with it."

Since Chad had a slight corneal abrasion, requiring application of artificial tears and ointment, the nurses assumed that he was uncomfortable, and that he wanted to complain. They wouldn't find out until the next day—when the respirator tube did come out—that true to form, what my wonderful son wanted to say was: "Thank you . . . thank you for giving me a new life."

As the high began to wear off, my thoughts turned in another direction—to a family somewhere nearby, who in the past twenty-four hours had lost one of its precious young members. Although we might never learn their names or meet them in person, we were told that for twenty-three years, Chad's new heart had powered the healthy body of a young woman, her life tragically ended by an automobile accident.

What horrendous emotions did that family have to deal with over the past twenty-four hours so that we could be on such a high? I wondered. I suddenly felt guilty for my happiness. It was almost Christmas, and this young woman's family had suffered the most devastating possible catastrophe—during the Season of Hope. What could I possibly do to ease their pain? How could I ever say "thank you"? It would be two months before I would be able to draft a note that even began to express our gratitude. In retrospect, I'm sure that even my carefully chosen words were inadequate either to communicate our appreciation or to decrease their despair.

As family members continued to trickle-in late that afternoon, each got to spend a few minutes visiting with Chad through the glass wall of his room. Since making Chad laugh had always been a family tradition, many came ready to raise his spirits. Had it been allowed by the hospital, I'm sure my mother would have brought her accordion and broken into some hand-clapping polka or Franco-American jig. But without her instrument handy, my mom resorted to her version of slapstick. She got a big chuckle out of Chad by taking out her teeth and flashing him a gummy smile.

But it was my brother Jim who drew the biggest smile from his nephew. In honor of their long-term adventure in competitive wind breaking, Jim opened a box and pulled out a T-shirt showing Michaelango's *God the Father*, from the Sistine Chapel, extending an index finger in creation.

On the Eighth Day, God Created the Winds, the shirt's caption read. And—according to the shirt's artist—the Almighty commanded: "Pull my finger."

CHAPTER SEVENTEEN: The Greatest Gift

I think of December 10 as my second birthday. Awakening in my room in Cardiac Intensive Care was as close to a rebirth as anyone probably gets.

Feeling that solid "thump" in my chest was awesome, an epic rush. For a tiny moment, I missed the *gwoosh* of my Fontan heart. But I got over it pretty quickly. I figured I was so used to it after seven years that not hearing it twisted my head around.

The breathing tube in my throat was bogus, but mostly because there was so much I wanted to say. There were so many people to thank, so much love to share. What made it okay was that for the first time in over a year, I wasn't struggling for air. Being able to breathe again was so wicked cool that the soreness in my chest from the incision seemed like no big deal. And there weren't even any new scars. My surgeon had been able to follow the old Fontan incision. Doc Del Nido was awesome.

The biggest mind-blower was my left arm. Ever since the subclavian steal surgery, that arm had looked and felt like a blueberry Popsicle—cold, purple and about as fat as a broomstick. The wound from my skateboarding accident had never really healed. It just got uglier.

As I watched my terrific family crowd themselves into the space outside my room, I couldn't help staring at that arm. It was pink; maybe with some oxygen, those muscles might even have a shot at pumping-up. I had worked hard at physical therapy after my second stroke, but with the lousy blood flow, I was just spinning my wheels.

My oxygen saturation was looking so awesome that they took the breathing tube out that first night after surgery. The rest of the family had already split, and only Mom and Brian were still hanging out in my room.

Just before they left for the night, Mom leaned over and whispered in my ear: "Chad, I wanted you to know that your new heart belonged to a young woman. She was twenty-three-years old. You have a very healthy heart that's almost the same age as your other organs. Isn't that wonderful?"

"Awesome, Mom," I said. Having a woman's heart was totally cool. I figured it might help me be a more sensitive dude. I fell asleep thanking God for allowing me to carry that wonderful woman's heart in my body.

♥ ♥ ♥

On Wednesday morning, December 11, I awoke from a totally peaceful dream. In the dream, I was sitting on a couch of blue crushed velvet in a huge room with a black-marble fireplace in which crackled a cozy fire. The ceiling was divided into small panels, each outlined by molding painted blue-gray. In every panel were scenes of boogying angels—looking like they were celebrating something. A central skylight of stained glass let sunlight into the room.

At the opposite end of the couch was a truly epic woman with deep brown eyes and shoulder-length brown hair. Around her head was a garland of flowers. Above her, there was a halo, fluffy-white like summer clouds.

Somehow, I knew this young woman was the donor of my new heart.

She smiled at me and said: "You're Chad, aren't you?"

"Chad, your mother's here," my nurse hollered from above my bed. "And it's time for your morning meds."

I opened my eyes to my room in Cardiac Intensive Care. Mom, Brian and Amy leaned over me. They were wearing masks and gowns.

"Who'd you bribe to let *you* in here," I said to my sister.

She frowned. "You really think I'd pay money to come see you?"

"Hey, why not, there's no one else like me."

"They said Amy could stay for a few minutes as long as she didn't touch you or get too close," Mom said.

"Boy, that's a relief, Mom," I said.

"I guess we're feeling chipper this morning, are we?" Mom asked.

I pointed to my eye. "It hurts, Mom. Can't they do anything."

The nurse answered the question: "The doctor said it's just a slight scratch on the cornea; there's no real infection. It should get better every day."

The nurse plopped two small containers on my bed tray. One was full of pills, the other had some milky yellow stuff. It was my first dance with the long list of new meds.

"The Vasotec and Cardura are to help take any strain off the new heart, let it slowly acclimate to its new body," the nurse said. "Then there's the anti-rejection meds . . . Cyclosporine, Solumedrol and Imuran. That leaves the anti-infectives . . . Bactrim and Mycostatin." She held up the cup of yellow liquid. "They're needed to protect you from bacteria and fungi . . . because of the suppression of your immune system by the anti-rejection drugs."

"Is that the whole menu?" I asked. "Doesn't sound real tasty. Any French fries come with that?"

"Sorry," she said, handing me the banana-colored stuff. "Please swish this one first . . . all around the inside of your mouth.

"Tastes like a watered-down Orange Julius," I said. "How 'bout an ice cream chaser?"

She smiled and shook her head.

"Can't I at least have some *real* juice?"

"Sorry, you'll get to start eating again tomorrow," the nurse said, helping me sip some water through a straw as I downed the endless lineup of pills after the Mycostatin swish.

"Good boy, Chad," the nurse said.

She turned toward my mother. "The doctor will be in to talk to you in just a few minutes."

Mom's body stiffened. "Is anything wrong?"

"Actually, he's doing just fine," Doctor Perry said, looping the last tie on his gown as he came into my room. Blood pressure and heart sounds are perfect. There's just one minor complication that we sometimes encounter."

As Mom squeezed Brian's hand, Doctor Perry explained that the donor—like many other people—had been a carrier of C.M.V.—Cytomegalovirus. Since I wasn't a carrier, the virus had been introduced into my body through the transplanted heart. That meant I'd have to get an extra drug for a few months, an anti-viral known as Gancyclovir. Plus, for about four months, I'd need a sort of vaccine against the virus to keep it from infecting cells of my other organs. This stuff was full of antibodies against the virus and went by the totally strange name of C.M.V. IgG.

Doc Perry lightly touched my sister's arm as he finished his explanation. "It would probably be best if you didn't spend any more time in here this morning."

"Aw, please; just a few more minutes," she said.

"Perhaps this afternoon," he said.

"What a whiner," I said. "It's a good thing I already bought your Christmas present two days before this all happened."

"Are you too out-of-it to tell me what it is?" Amy asked.

"No way, I'm not tellin' . . . get outta here," I said.

"Can you tell *me*?" the nurse said, coming closer to the bed.

"Hey, give me a break, okay. My lips are sealed," I said.

As my sister left the room, I spotted two dudes outside. The first was my dad, looking like he needed some sleep.

The second guy looked familiar, but I couldn't place him. He wore a short white coat, had a dark brown complexion, bulging eyes and a big bright smile. He carried an I.V. bag. His nametag said "Rolf Alphonse R.Ph.," but it didn't activate any sectors in my memory stores; not right away.

A pharmacist—maybe he knows my Aunt Ann, I thought. Then, I heard his jolly voice, and it all came together.

"Mister Chad, it's great to see you," the pharmacist said. "You lookin' good, bro. . . for someone just spent ten hours in the O.R."

Suddenly, it was 1985 again, and I was a little kid, tightly wrapped in my orange life jacket, speeding along on my grandfather's boat with some of my family and a bunch of students from Ann's pharmacy school. Everybody was laughing while they hooted and put their hands together for Rolf. Rolf didn't swim and he'd never water-skied. But he rock-and-rolled around that lake—with his eyes closed and a flipped-out look on his face. He stayed on those skis and never let go.

Now, God had sent this friend of my family's to make sure my intravenous drugs were totally together, high-voltage. It was another one of those *coincidences* that made all of us feel so awesome about the transplant.

My doctors finally let me start eating on Thursday the

12th. Of course, it was hospital food, but I did get to choose my menu, and that grilled cheese sandwich tasted as good as anything I had ever eaten. After lunch, I was allowed to get out of bed and take short walks around my room. There was no dizziness, no shortness of breath, nothing but the smooth thump-thump-thump that I was quickly getting used to as the new drum inside my body. I thought about what my friend Owen had said: "Like night and day."

I got to go for a longer walk—outside my room—on Friday the 13th. I blew-off all the "bad luck" hype, and it was a great day for me. Doc Perry told us that my numbers looked good enough to transfer me out of Intensive Care as soon as a room became available.

They did transfer me to 6-East that weekend, just five days after surgery. It was great to be out of the fish tank. With every hour, every meal and every step, my body was feeling stronger, and I started thinking about being home for Christmas.

♥ ♥ ♥

On Thursday, the 19th, Doctor Smoot came back to the hospital from a conference. She found my mother talking to my nurses at the Sixth-floor station.

"I hear we have a transplant," Doctor Smoot said. Smiling, she walked toward my room. Mom later told me that everybody on that floor had their binoculars on Doctor Smoot. Nobody could believe their eyes. Her hair was royal blue.

When she came into my room, Doctor Smoot did a little fashion-model turn to make sure I got a good look.

"I understand that someone's got a beautiful healthy heart pumping smoothly inside him," she said.

"Yup, that would be me, doc." I winked.

"Sorry about the color, Chad," she said. "I couldn't find any purple in the temporary stuff . . . and if I don't wash this out by tomorrow, they'll probably ask for my resignation."

"Hey, the blue's awesome, Doctor Smoot," I said. I stroked my own hair. "I kinda even like it better than my blond."

"Glad you approve. I'll make sure that my secretary, Kim, gives you the rest of the bottle before we kick you out of here tomorrow."

"Tomorrow!"

"Sure! Your mom said your family's celebrating Christmas together this weekend. Don't you want to be there?"

"Heck yes," I said. "I'm psyched."

"Good, we've already changed your Solumedrol to oral prednisone, and the nurses will carefully go over your meds with you and your mom."

"I'll do whatever you say," I said.

"Good," she said. "But you'll need to be back here Tuesday—that's Christmas Eve—for your first diagnostic biopsy. Deal?"

"Deal."

"By the way, Kim says you guys like the same kind of music. She wanted me to tell you that she knows a band called *The Queers*."

"No stuff . . . they're an awesome band . . . outta Portsmouth, New Hampshire."

"I'm pretty confident you'll be feeling well enough to go to one of their concerts really soon, Chad."

I squeezed her hand. "Thanks, Doctor Smoot . . . thanks for everything." She was so cool. I didn't know what else to say.

I had prayed for three things for Christmas: a new heart,

a turntable to listen to my collection of independent music produced on vinyl, and a guitar amplifier. All of a sudden, the material stuff seemed bogus. I had a new life and I'd be home for the family Christmas. What a rush!

♥ ♥ ♥

When I arrived home on Friday night, December 20th, I was greeted in my room by a huge piece of cardboard. Decorated in black paint and lettered with silver-metal rectangles glued end-to-end, it declared: "We ♥ Chad."

My friends had gone to lots of trouble to make me a punk card that would let me know how much my health meant to them. I was blown-away by the emotion. *It wouldn't matter if there was nothing under the tree with my name on it,* I thought. Yet, when I looked over at my music equipment, I saw the turntable. My awesome parents couldn't resist.

Turning my head toward a figure in the doorway of my room, I saw my sister, Amy. She had just gotten home from college for the holiday recess.

I smiled and pointed to the turntable. "Check it out, Ames; look what Mom and Brian got me."

She threw her arms around me. "Check it out, Chad, God gave me the best Christmas present I could ever hope to get." She hugged me tighter and kissed my cheek. "It wouldn't have mattered if you had totally blown-off buying me a gift."

I always knew my sister loved me, but until that moment, I don't think I knew just how much.

My memory of that Sunday, December 22 family-Christmas gathering is hazy. I remember the beautiful tree in my Aunt Claire and Uncle Bob's family room, but I spent most of the time looking at it through my own tears of joy. The specifics—the gifts, the food, my grandmother and uncles trying to out-bellow one another to a Christmas-carol Karaoke video—are mostly a blur. I was too choked-up to catch it all.

But I *was* tuned-in to how that day *felt*. For I totally realized why I had wanted the transplant; why it was so important to live. All these people loved me, and I loved them all so much, too. It was the best reason to celebrate a new life—the only real reason. I thought of all the people who couldn't enjoy Christmas because they were sick, and of all the physically healthy people for whom Christmas was still empty because they had no one to love them. At that moment, I had no doubt that I was one of the luckiest people on earth.

CHAPTER EIGHTEEN:
A Patient Christmas

This time, we were walking hand-in-hand in a snow-covered field. Big puffy snowflakes hovered just over her head, forming a crystal white halo.

"How do you feel, Chad?" she said softly, her brown eyes shining like spotlights.

"I feel awesome," I said. "And I had a great family Christmas yesterday."

She nodded. "You're going to be fine; there may be a few bumps here and there, but you're going to be fine." She walked into a grove of Christmas spruce and disappeared.

When I opened my eyes to my sunny bedroom, the first thing I saw was the giant welcome-home card from my friends. It was a great way to start the day.

Glancing at the clock, I jumped out of bed. I remembered that my home-health-care nurses would be coming to check my vitals and juice me with anti-viral meds.

For a minute, my mind played a trick on me. I expected to feel *weesh*: dizzy and short of breath. But those feelings were history. My new heart was solid. I stood up and started moving around my room.

Before too much of the day got away from us, Mom made me sit down and listen to the messages on the answering machine. There was one really important one she wanted me to hear.

The audio sounded like a prehistoric P.A. system with

static piped-in from a satellite. But it didn't matter. I still got the message loud and clear.

"Chad; this is Doctor McFaul calling from Mexico," the voice said. "Congratulations on your new heart. I wanted you to know how pleased I am for you . . . and how much you deserve it. I'm confident that you're finally going to have the better life you've been waiting for . . . for so long. A very Merry Christmas to you and your family."

Those words really made my day. For three months, I had been totally ticked at Doctor McFaul, feeling that the man I had depended on for my whole life had all of a sudden blown me off. When I saw how depressed my mom looked at the news that Doctor McFaul was leaving, it made me feel really hateful toward him. It was a feeling that didn't come naturally to me, and it got me really twisted inside. The message from Mexico changed a lot of that. I realized that Doctor McFaul had never really abandoned me in spirit. He still cared about me as much as he had during our sixteen years together.

My first hint that life wasn't just going to be a total cakewalk came about an hour later when the visiting nurses arrived. As they checked me over, they found a rash on my back. After *spazzing* through their diagnosis books and consulting with my Aunt Ann, they decided it was probably a reaction to the prednisone. They phoned Children's, but since I'd be going in for my biopsy the next day, no one seemed too bent out of shape, and I still got my dose of anti-viral drugs.

It would be a few weeks before I'd have to deal with the bogus side-effects of the prednisone. The moon face and thickening of my neck might have been cool if I'd played linebacker for the E.L.H.S. football team. But since I was about five-ten, one-fifty, my new look was truly strange.

♥ ♥ ♥

I guess I needed a wake-up call before I zoned-in on how important the prednisone and the other anti-rejection meds were to my body. That message zonked me on Christmas Eve, just two weeks after my transplant.

"Bet you're not happy to see this place again so soon," Mom said, as she pulled the car up the circular driveway of Children's.

"It's okay, Mom; I'm psyched to see Lisa and Stacy and the other nurses, and . . . " I pointed to my royal-blue hair, " . . . Doctor Smoot."

Coming back to Children's with blue hair was sort of my way of saying "thank you" again to the doctors and nurses. After all, if it's your biological family that gives you life, then—by giving me my second life—these guys had to be my second family.

I was taken directly to the cath lab where Doc Perry was waiting. The lighting in the room was alien. It came from a bank of video monitors, one of which followed the catheter through my veins.

Doc Perry would later be in *Boston Magazine*, as one of the best doctors in the area, and it was easy to see why.

"Just give my hand a tight squeeze, Chad," he said. "And don't worry, I'm not going to hurt you."

"No problem, Doc Perry," I said.

"Now twist your head that way . . . good. Just a little lidocaine and then you'll feel some pressure."

That was about it, the needle was in my vein, and Doctor Perry began to thread the tiny tube through it—the catheter, which would snake its way into my heart, where a tiny piece of tissue would be snipped from the inside. With Doctor Perry's awesome skill, it was all over in less than twenty minutes.

They wheeled me up to a room in Six East where Mom and I waited for the results.

"That color blue looks better on you than it does on me, Chad." Doctor Smoot sounded like everything was cool, but I could see the heavy lyrics in her face. I flashed her a big smile to let her know that I wasn't going to get twisted, no matter what; that I was hanging in there.

"Is the heart still okay, Doctor Smoot?" Mom asked with a *spazz* in her voice.

"The numbers look fine, Mrs. Boily . . . and it sounds great on the echo."

Mom relaxed and sank back into her chair.

"Unfortunately, there *is* a small amount of white blood cell infiltration into the heart muscle," Doctor Smoot said. "It's a sign that Chad's immune system is recognizing that the heart's not his own."

Mom's face went white. "Oh God, it's being rejected," she gasped.

Doctor Smoot put a hand on Mom's shoulder. "It's the earliest sign of an impending rejection event. It's exactly why we do the biopsies . . . to catch it early."

Mom started breathing again. "What do we do now?"

"We treat it aggressively by adding more anti-rejection drugs. Naturally we'll have to keep him here for a few days and do another biopsy."

Christmas in the hospital—it flipped-out my sister and some other people in my family a lot more than it did me. I had already had my Christmas and my Christmas present. If my doctors and nurses were willing to treat me on Christmas, then I was totally willing to help them get it done.

They transferred me to a pressurized room, so germs wouldn't float in every time the door was opened. Because I needed more anti-rejection drugs, my immune system wouldn't be kicking too much butt for a while. That was cool for my new heart, but it let the germs off the hook, too.

True to form, Mom did her best to make it feel like Christmas. She brought in a tree that she stuck near the bathroom door of my room. On Christmas morning, after my aunt and uncle visited, Mom and I wrapped a bunch of gifts that we handed-out to the kids on the ward. It made me think of Alex and the magic shows that I had put together after my Fontan surgery. But this was almost better. It was Christmas, and any kid who had to spend it in the hospital deserved to have some reason to smile.

I didn't get left out. Back in my room, I found a chair full of gifts. As Doctor Smoot had promised, her secretary, Kim, had brought a whole pile of great stuff from *The Queers*. There were autographed publicity pics and copies of all their CDs. But most important, there was a hand-written note telling me to hang-in-there and get well, so I could come to their next concert.

A few days later, a second biopsy of my heart showed that my white blood cells had backed off. For the time being, I'd have to come back for a biopsy every two weeks. But I also knew that in time, they would get less frequent. The new year was close-by, and it was time to start really living the first year of my new life.

EPILOGUE:
Long and Winding Road

"*H*ow's your nephew doing?"

Since Chad's heart transplant, I have answered that question literally hundreds of times.

Thankfully, in most instances, I've been able to answer very positively: "He's doing great."

Although he still occasionally must serve as "practice dummy" for novice cardiology residents, Chad has mostly had a succession of clean biopsies. The heart itself continues to function beautifully, and Chad now participates in skateboarding and bicycle riding, no longer merely the "video-man."

Despite a junior year of high school spent primarily at home or in the hospital, he remarkably managed to finish his course work on time. Unfortunately, his hiatus from school was not limited solely to the pre-transplant hospitalizations, since his health suffered a serious, though not completely unanticipated setback during the spring of 1997.

It began with headaches and continued with his inability to breathe through his nose and taste his food. In one sense, the diagnosis was straightforward. A C.T. scan revealed an abnormal growth in his nasal passages. But the more important questions represented great cause for concern:

What was the source of this growth? And were there other growths elsewhere in his body?

The physicians called it P.T.L.D.—"Post Transplant Lymphatic Disorder," and for the sake of Chad and his immediate family, I was grateful that they had access to the euphemism. It sounded a lot better than "lymphoma."

The plain fact was that Chad had grown a B-Lymphoma, a tumor originating from a normal type of white blood cell important to his immune system. In a letter to Doctor Hourihan of May 15,1997, Doctor Smoot explained the data suggesting that Epstein-Barr Virus—more casually known to scientists as E.B.V.—had precipitated Chad's nasopharyngeal tumor.

It is known that many people carry the silent DNA of E.B.V. in their cells. Occasionally, the virus becomes active, stimulating cell multiplication. In normal individuals, such an event can be free of overt consequences, the abnormal cells and virus eliminated by an otherwise healthy immune system. However, in someone taking a cocktail of immunosuppressive drugs to prevent heart-transplant rejection, the results can be devastating.

As we awaited the results of Chad's tests, I couldn't help but hear my sister-in-law's voice ringing in my brain. "At least, thank God, it's not cancer," Louise would frequently say as a form of self-encouragement during the sixteen-year ordeal of Chad's cardiovascular illness. It was her way of expressing that she *did* have a sick child, but that there were other children—children tragically stricken with cancer—who were even sicker. I prayed, for her sake as much as for Chad's, that after everything they had been through together, cancer would not, could not be their final destiny.

Fortunately, the tumor was surgically removed without complications, and subsequent C.T. and Gallium scans were negative. Chad was, thank God, free of metastasizing (cancerous) tumors. The anti-viral drug, Zovirax, was added to his already formidable array of medications.

"Stay off the Internet," Doctor Smoot told my sister-in-law. It was a warning to isolate herself from viral horror stories that infected the digital signals coursing over those phone lines, but which were mostly irrelevant to Chad's future. It was great advice from a wonderful source, a woman who had demonstrated her affection and regard for her patient and his family in so many ways. I do believe that it was only partially tongue-in-cheek when, in a letter to Doctor Hourihan, Doctor Smoot wrote: "I look forward to following Chad with you but regret that I won't be able to emulate his latest hair color."

The tumor growth was a signal from Chad's immune system to his physicians, informing them that they needed to readjust his level of anti-rejection drugs. The task was, in principle, a daunting one. They would need to achieve a delicate balance whereby Chad's immune system would, in the future, be potent enough to prevent such tumors from growing, yet not so potent as to reject the heart that was his key to a normal life.

Thankfully, this has—at least for the present—been accomplished. Against a backdrop of normal biopsies, Chad has shown no repeat incidence of the tumor episode. And by contrast to his tortuous medical history, his surgery to correct an inguinal hernia during the late summer of 1997 seemed remarkably mundane.

"His heart is better than most of ours," one of the staff nurses was heard to remark, as she examined the cardiac monitor in post-op. Three days after the hernia repair, Chad was back in Maine at his summer job.

♥ ♥ ♥

Chad spent his senior year actively engaged in the college application process, and he was accepted to several schools of his choosing. During that same period, he managed to work two jobs, both of which involved public interaction and which demonstrated the significant emotional maturity that grew out of his long illness. His sister, Amy, recommended him for one of the jobs, a stint as a retail-store associate.

"I felt completely comfortable recommending him," Amy revealed, "because of the changes in the way we interact as brother and sister. Sure we still argue occasionally, but mostly, we air our grievances . . . then talk things out . . . without any name-calling or finger-pointing."

Amy adds: "I hope Chad gets into the public liaison aspect of healthcare. There's such a need there for people who like to communicate one-on-one, and that's what Chad's really excellent at. Just think of what he has to offer. My God, he lived two lifetimes in sixteen years."

I was particularly impressed with a story related by Brian, to whom Chad increasingly refers as his "step-dad." Two months after the transplant, Brian had an unexplained bout of illness, and he underwent a series of G.I. tests over a several day period. During that time, Chad had his first overnight stay away from home since well before the onset of his pre-transplant heart failure. He was, at the time, being introduced to a new group of friends in Falmouth, Maine, an hour's drive from home. Despite his hectic social schedule and the importance of a diversity of peer interaction to someone who had literally been a prisoner of his illness for over six months, Chad managed to think of his step-dad that evening.

"Chad? Is anything wrong?" Brian naturally reacted after answering the phone.

"No, everything's cool," Chad said.

"Do you need a ride or anything?" Brian asked.

"Nope. Just called because I wanted to find out about your tests," Chad said. "I was worried about you . . . you okay?"

"Yeah, I'll live; it's no big deal. But thanks for calling. I really appreciate it," Brian said.

Chad's "two lifetimes" of interpersonal experience will undoubtedly serve him well, whatever his chosen career. Yet for all his maturity, there are still a few boyish aspects to his personality that may appear to represent immature regressions. In reality, most of them boil down to unfulfilled aspirations, stifled fancies, whimsies muted by the strange and unhealthy *gwoosh* of a patched-together heart.

"I'm gonna skate, Mom . . . I'm gonna learn. And someday I'm gonna shoot a puck into the net past Jimmy," Chad, at one point, announced to my sister-in-law.

As competitive a goalie as he is, Jimmy would nonetheless be thrilled at the privilege of allowing that particular goal, I thought. Any of us would be.

Chad graduated Edward Little High School in June of 1998. That fall, he began his freshman year at Manhattanville College.

POSTSCRIPT:
Spreading the Word

*A*fter his transplant, Chad gave the keynote address at several events, ranging from a Rotary Club luncheon to the yearly fund-raising march of his local chapter of the American Heart Association. Following is the text of a 1997 speech:

My name is Chad Boily. I'm a seventeen-year-old senior at Edward Little High School. The reason I can be here today to speak to all of you is because of the generous gift of life given to me by a donor family. I had a heart transplant this past December and now feel I have a chance at a new life.

I was born with a serious congenital heart defect. Not much could be done to repair the inside of my heart at that time, but at about one month of age, I had my first heart operation. Much work was done on the outside of my heart; repairing my aorta and placing a band on my pulmonary artery. There were many visits to the cardiologist and many cardiac catheterizations performed during those years to keep track of the functions within my heart. In those early years, whenever I got a cold, there was a threat of pneumonia. When I got sick, there usually was a hospital stay. My childhood wasn't the best, because I was very limited and not able to do what a lot of kids my age could do.

As time progressed, I began to tire more easily. At age

eight, my doctor started to be concerned with my lack of energy, so he suggested that we look into a procedure called the "Fontan." This operation was done at Children's Hospital in Boston, and it involved the dividing of my heart into three functioning chambers. My left ventricle was badly deformed, so they redirected my arteries to improve my circulation. At age nine, the surgery was performed. After being at Children's Hospital for two months or more, I came home feeling I had bought more time.

I was home for about two weeks when, one day at the dinner table, my arm suddenly dropped and went completely numb. We called our doctor and he checked me out and felt I should return to Boston and be re-evaluated and put on blood thinners. Things were better for a while after this.

A short time after, I began to experience serious headaches, and in some cases, I experienced some strange episodes of car sickness. It was a short time after these episodes that I experienced a stroke that affected my right side. Luckily, it was detected early enough that with the help of occupational therapy and physical therapy, I was able to regain nearly full range of motion within a year.

The summer of 1992, school had just ended; we were three days into summer vacation. My uncle took me to a Red Sox game. I began to feel sharp pains in my abdomen that evening. The next morning, the pain increased, and my mom took me to the hospital, and sure enough, my appendix was ready to rupture. I had surgery, and one week later, on the day I was to be discharged, I suffered a second, more serious stroke. I was rushed to Portland where numerous studies were done. No one could understand why I had another stroke. This stroke has since left me with weakness on my left side. Many tests were done and it was found that there was a blood steal occurring at the brainstem; probably due to poor circulation. The suggestion was to undergo surgery for another procedure to band an artery in my arm. I spent seven weeks in the hospital that summer and, believe me, that is not how any kid wants to spend his or her summer vacation. Things were better for a few years after that, but I found myself getting tired again.

Last summer is when it really hit me. I began to experience chronic fatigue. I also found myself very limited as to what I could do. A visit to the doctor determined that my heart was, in fact, failing. This came as a shock to both my family and me. What really surprised me was when my doctor came in and told me that he could do nothing for me in Portland, that I would have to go to Boston. When I went to Boston, I was visited and tested by several doctors. It seemed to boil down to only one solution. That's when they told me I needed a heart transplant. Overwhelmed by the situation we were in, we began to learn all about heart transplants. At the beginning of October, I was officially listed for a heart transplant.

At that time, because my heart was failing so quickly, I found myself in the hospital almost every two weeks. I would be placed in the Intensive Care Unit, where they would administer medicine called Amrinone to help recharge my heart. Those weeks were very long and depressing. During that time, I had the fortunate opportunity to meet a few people who had had heart transplants, and their visits gave me the courage to keep hoping. I was sent home with a long distance beeper. It was mentioned several times that I could die while waiting.

With God's help and the support of family and friends, I never lost hope. It took seventy-two long days to finally get the call. On December ninth, I received the call of a lifetime. They had found a suitable donor. It would be extremely difficult for me to express to you how I felt at that moment. Within an hour of that call, we were en route to

Boston.

The eight-hour surgery was performed at four in the morning on December tenth. Although it was a difficult procedure, I made it through. The surgery was successful. I was out of the hospital ten days after the transplant. I was fortunate enough to receive a twenty-three-year-old female heart. It is tough to describe the feelings that go through you when you know a family has to suffer a tragedy in order for you to gain a chance at life, and it is for this reason, I will be eternally grateful to the donor family. God bless them all.

Today, I feel like a totally different person. My energy level is like it's never been before. Everything I do, even simple things like eating, breathing, and even speaking, are better. Unlike the past, I have no more limitations. I have to take medicine for the rest of my life, but that's a small price to pay for a chance at a new life. I return to Boston for periodic biopsies to check for rejection. I don't know what I would have done without the skilled, knowledgeable doctors at Boston's Children's Hospital. I will be watched closely for at least the first year. It is wonderful to be able to hope and dream again, to have fun with my family and friends, and to plan for the future.

I don't know what your feelings are when it comes to organ donation, but if you at any time have considered becoming a donor, please do so. If not, I hope my story will help persuade you all to become organ donors. There is a great need.

Thank you.